A KEY TO MODERN ENGLISH POETRY

BY

MARTIN GILKES, M.C., M.A.

BLACKIE & SON LIMITED
LONDON AND GLASGOW

BLACKIE & SON LIMITED
66 Chandos Place, London
17 Stanhope Street, Glasgow

BLACKIE & SON (INDIA) LIMITED
103/5 Fort Street, Bombay

BLACKIE & SON (CANADA) LIMITED
Toronto

THE PAPER AND BINDING OF THIS BOOK CONFORM TO THE AUTHORIZED ECONOMY STANDARDS

To

DENNE

and

MICKLEJOHN

Printed in Great Britain by Blackie & Son, Ltd., Glasgow

FOREWORD TO SECOND EDITION

This book was written in 1937, some considerable time ago. The publication of a second edition might be thought a good opportunity of bringing it up to date and including poets who are writing at the present time. I do not think so. It would be entirely contrary to the purpose for which the book was written. It was never meant, as I was careful to state in the first chapter, either as a textbook or a kind of year book, in which the name of any poet writing now can be looked up and a short account of his career be found together with a few lines of criticism. The book was written with a different and specific purpose. It was intended to point out and discuss the root causes of the differences which everyone must notice between the poetry of the twentieth century and the poetry of a period immediately preceding it. Those causes still remain operative.

Some of the poets mentioned in the book are alive and writing still. Some have added to their reputations, others have not. T. S. Eliot has abandoned the attempt to reproduce the general social reaction to the period in which we are living, as in "Waste Land", for the profundities of his own personal attitude towards the world in which he finds himself ("East Coker" and "The Dry Salvages", for instance). He has added greatly to his already great reputation. Not so perhaps Ezra Pound, whose latinity for instance has been found wanting, though the influence which a writer has had upon the literary movements of his day remains, whatever the quality of his writing may be: and Pound in his younger days was certainly an influence of considerable importance.

"The War", when the book was written, was the conflict which began in 1914 and finished in 1918. Since that time we have just passed through another period of war in which the difficulties and sufferings have been even greater and have, in addition, very deeply affected the inhabitants of every nation in the world.

It was Wordsworth who defined poetry as "Emotion recollected in tranquillity". As a definition it is somewhat incomprehensive, but as a statement of naked fact it is wholly admirable. No man, in actual moments of excitement, can put down on paper satisfactorily the excitement which he feels and relate it properly to the good and bad of human life as he has himself considered and experienced it. I have described in one chapter the effect of war upon the poetry of our time. The result of the last five years has been exactly the same, only more so. The Bodley Head published a volume of modern "Air Force Poetry". In a review in the *Sunday Times* during August, 1944, Stephen Spender said of it that "Most of the poems are not finished works of art, they are frantic messages and violent notes of experiences which have crashed down upon the author's head." In other words, there has been no tranquillity in which to relate the poets' emotion to the length and breadth of human life. This is profoundly true. One has only to examine the book to see it clearly for oneself. I have therefore made no amplification or alteration in my chapter on the effect of 1914 to 1918 upon English Poetry. In my opinion none is needed and I let the book stand as it was written.

MARTIN GILKES

August, 1944.

CONTENTS

What is that, mother?
That, dear, is a wood.
Can we go in?
Yes, if you like.
What's this, mother?
That's a tree, dear.
And this? And this? And this?
All trees, dear.
And this?
That's a tree, too, I think, only it has run a little wild.
Oh mother, where's the wood gone to?
It's still here, dearest. We are in it; but you can't see it for the trees.

From *Micklejohn's Instructional Album.*

A Key to Modern English Poetry

PROLOGUE

A KEY is neither an Inventory nor a Catalogue; neither is it an Essay in Criticism nor any of a hundred other things. A key has a simpler purpose. It unlocks a room—in this case the room of Modern Poetry—and provides a general view of what is inside from a strategic position at the door. It is a strategic position. For it enables you to recognize similarities and trace broad lines of development much more easily than you could if you were actually inside the room—just as an aeroplane gives a better idea of the contours of an ancient earthwork than any amount of tramping over it with notebook and compass.

The purpose of this book is to provide that kind of general view: the broad lines on which Modern Poetry has developed. Therefore I have not attempted to notice every poet included in a modern Anthology, or even every modern poet of distinction. Once inside the room—forewarned and forearmed (that is, knowing in advance what to expect there)—anyone can make acquaintance with whom he likes: and if he doesn't like, can pass on.

Inside the room, too, there are to be found plenty of guides, both amateur and official, who will be delighted either to instruct the inquirer's ignorance or take him on a personally conducted tour. Some are sprightly, some are unbelievably portentous, and all speak with authority (especially when the one contradicts the other); but to get the best out of them (and at times even to understand properly what they have to tell you), you need, I think, to be familiar with the inside of the room and the conventions of language which are in force there. Modern Poetry is considered "difficult"; modern criticism, even when not written by the poets themselves, on occasion can make scarcely less difficult reading. For instance, here is a sentence from Mr. Michael Roberts' Preface to *The Faber Book of Modern Verse*: "Sometimes several of these terminologies are superimposed, serving as metaphors for each other, and concentrating, intensifying and ultimately simplifying the problems by this poetic identification." What is the ordinary reader to make of this? At first glance must it not seem as difficult as one of Torquemada's celebrated cross-words? And one could cap it with no more trouble than turning a page—or picking up another critic at random. Take this from Mr. Empson's *Seven Types of Ambiguity*: "In analysing the statement made by a sentence (having, no doubt, fixed on the statement by an apprehension of the implications of the sentence) one would continually be dealing with a sort of ambiguity due to metaphors . . ." and so on. The complete sentence runs to four more lines.

Both these extracts of course do mean something—and something quite precise and definite. Even without their contexts that should be clear; but to achieve their meaning the ordinary reader must make a considerable mental effort. Good will is not enough: he needs both agility and stamina. Could not Mr. Roberts, he may well ask, have said all that he wants to say in words more nearly of one syllable? And need Mr. Empson have given us such a Henry James of a sentence?

But no. There is a convention of language inside the room; and once inside, the reader very quickly becomes accustomed to it. Indeed, he must; for practically every one of our modern critics adopts it on occasion.[1] It is not altogether the schoolmaster's itch for preaching, a weakness from which we are none of us wholly free. It is due equally, I think, to a feeling that one can only express oneself with real precision and accuracy in the new words and manner which Science has introduced into our language during the last thirty years or so. Not that they are not good words. They are both precise and comprehensive, new shining and efficient monsters, like our modern machines; and to express certain new things and certain complex new ideas, they are necessary. On the other hand, they have had the effect of making a good deal of modern critical writing seem like extracts from a scientific textbook.

This book stands upon the threshold. I have tried to avoid as far as possible the textbook language of Science, and I have tried to escape the schoolmaster's itch. I have not intended more than a sketch from the doorway (an aeroplane view) of the beginning and

[1] There are certain notable exceptions. For example, Mr. Edmund Wilson's *Axel's Castle*, which "traces the origins of certain tendencies in contemporary literature" in a style of crystal clarity, and makes a complicated subject (the Symbolists and their influence) seem almost as simple as A.B.C.

subsequent development of Modern English Poetry: so that at the end the reader may advance into the room with a broad and general idea of what he will find there.

CHAPTER I

Plus ça Change

I ONCE heard a preacher expounding a knotty point of doctrine.

"My friends," he declared at the conclusion of his discourse, "it is indeed no easy idea which I have been putting to you. It is both vague and definite, like that curious oddity, the jellyfish. See it swimming in the sea (if the Almighty has given jellyfishes the power to swim), or lying extended on the shore: and which of us would be prepared to say exactly where the creature begins and ends? Yet it is no illusion. It is real, it exists. Put your foot upon it, my friends, and (my goodness!) you know that it is there!"

He might perhaps have expressed himself better, but what he meant is clear enough: and it applies, I think, with equal point to modern poetry. Everyone recognizes that there is some such thing and, if given time, I do not suppose many would have any difficulty in quoting an example: but to define its limits, to say exactly where the creature begins and ends, is a very different matter.

What, in fact, do we mean by modern poetry? Do we mean the poetry written within the last five, ten or fifteen years? or do we mean all the poetry written since the War, 1914–18? But a glance at any anthology will show that actually during that war, especially towards the end of it, some poetry, at any rate, was being written which fairly deserves the name of "modern".

And perhaps we ought to go even further back and make the first years of the century our dividing line.

There still remains another alternative. Would it not be better to distinguish by personalities rather than by dates? Dates always look so well on paper, but in practice more often than not they only serve to confuse the issue. Take, for instance, that solid and important date, 1918, when the War ended and the post-War era with all its troubles began. Supposing we say that "modern" poetry is poetry written since 1918, some very odd contradictions will result. To take only one—in 1929 Robert Bridges published his *Testament of Beauty*: but seven years earlier, in 1922, T. S. Eliot's *The Waste Land* had appeared. Now whatever may be thought of *The Testament of Beauty*—and it is surely too considerable a poem to be passed by with a shrug or dismissed (in Dr. Leavis' phrase) as "a disquisition in verse that is scholarly and original, but dead"—it can hardly be called "modern" in the sense in which *The Waste Land* is modern. Bridges' poem is the swan-song of a late-Victorian. It is the final word of an old man looking out upon the strange new world around him and rationalizing what he sees in the light of his own established and matured philosophy. He faces both present and future, but all the while himself remains securely rooted in the past, so that for him it is the new order that must be reconciled with the old, not the old with the new. But *The Waste Land* is entirely different. It has no sort of affinity with what has gone before. The break is complete. It turns its back deliberately upon tradition and the old methods and the old manner. It is "modern" to its finger-tips—so modern, in fact, as to make *The*

Testament of Beauty appear quite ancient by comparison.

Such then is the value of dates. We cannot lay down any definite period within which all the poetry written may be counted as "modern" in contrast to the poetry of an earlier date: nor indeed is it possible to fix any definite "Year One" of the new era. Our criterion can only be the poet himself. His mind is what matters. Is he forward- or backward-looking? Has he the modern outlook?

And this question, of course, immediately suggests another (or rather two questions which are really one). What is this "modern" outlook, and what do forward- and backward-looking mean?

Perhaps a quotation will help towards the answer. "The great rising tide of the modern mind, which . . . overturned the whole edifice of human conditions and speculations." Has not this a vaguely familiar ring? It might come from almost any recent book on the state of literature to-day. It might be Mr. Day Lewis writing in *A Hope for Poetry*:[1] it might be Mr. Michael Roberts in his Preface to *New Signatures*:[2] it might (except for a certain staidness of expression) be Mr. Geoffrey Grigson in the pages of that stimulating little paper, *New Verse*. It might indeed be any one of a dozen. Actually it is nothing of the kind. Up-to-date though it sounds, it is nevertheless a voice from the middle of the last century. The text is taken from the first chapter of the fourth book of the great French critic Taine's *History of English Literature*.[3]

That critical work was published in 1863; and, I

[1] *A Hope for Poetry*, Cecil Day Lewis (Oxford, Basil Blackwell).

[2] *New Signatures*, (Hogarth Living Poets, No. 24).

[3] *Histoire de la Littérature Anglaise*, H. A. Taine, trans. van Laun.

think, most readers to-day must be a little surprised at such a reference at such a date as that to "the modern mind" which upset all orthodox standards and played havoc with conventional ideas. Taine's words so exactly express our situation to-day that one might wonder whether perhaps he intended a prophecy. Was he by any chance making an inspired Wellsian guess at the shape of things to come? He was not, of course. A *History of English Literature* is not an Old Moore's *Almanac* or a sibylline book that draws the veil from the face of the future. He was looking, not forward, but back to the early years of his own century and sketching the outlines of the strange exciting brand-new world which was then just coming into being. In other words, he was describing the birth of the Victorian Era: and in particular the revolutionary change that came over poetry at that time.

Looking back from our vantage-point of the mid-twentieth century we are not accustomed to think of the nineteenth century either as exciting or revolutionary or modern. Indeed the epithets we generally apply to it are exactly the opposite. We are inclined to think of it and all its works as distinctly *vieux jeu*, like an intermediate stop when the train has passed it on a railway journey. But compare it with the period which immediately preceded it: set the impulsive warmth of the Romantics against the impersonal formality of the Era of Classical Perfection (could there be a contrast more abrupt?)—and Taine's language becomes more understandable. Far from being dull, settled and conventional, the early years of the nineteenth century were in reality just as full of change, uncertainty and excitement as the period through which we have passed since 1918. There was a new movement in poetry then, exactly as there is to-day: and it was equally shocking to an older generation, which could not shake itself free from the traditions and inhibitions of the Past. For then, as now, the new poetry was in violent opposition to what had gone before. It had broken away and was adventuring along what were then entirely new lines. The difference between Eliot and Tennyson, if you compare without prejudice, is no greater and no more radical than the difference between Byron and Pope.

And the similarity goes further. It does not extend, of course, to the type of poetry which the two movements produced. Out of the early nineteenth century came, in the fullness of time, all that poetry which we now know by the name of Victorian; and no one needs to be told how little the Victorian poets resemble our modern poets of to-day! But the mainspring which set both movements in motion, the revolutionary slogan which inspired the pioneers, was in both cases —odd though it may seem—precisely the same.

We can almost fix a definite date for the beginning of the earlier movement. In 1798 Wordsworth and Coleridge published a joint collection of poems under the title of *Lyrical Ballads*: and to the second edition Wordsworth added a Preface which was to all intents and purposes a Manifesto. " I am sensible that there would be something like impropriety in abruptly obtruding upon the public, without a few words of introduction, Poems so materially different from those upon which general approbation is at present bestowed."[1] And he proceeds both to justify poetry in

[1] Preface, *Lyrical Ballads*, 2nd Edition.

breaking away from established tradition and to set forth what the form and the aim of the new poetry should be. Consider the following extracts. The voice is the voice of Wordsworth, but is not the substance of what he says exactly what our modern Poets are saying and have been saying about themselves ever since the present new movement originated?

"Those who have been accustomed to the gaudiness and inane phraseology of many modern writers, if they persist in reading this book . . . , will, no doubt, have to struggle with feelings of strangeness and awkwardness: they will look round for poetry, and will be induced to inquire by what species of courtesy these attempts can be permitted to assume that title.

"The principal object, then, proposed (in this kind of poetry) was to choose incidents and situations from common life, and to relate them, throughout, as far as was possible in a selection of language really used by men.

"My purpose was to imitate and, as far as possible, to adopt the very language of men, . . . I have wished to keep the Reader in the company of flesh and blood, persuaded that by so doing I shall interest him. . . . Consequently there will be found in these volumes little of what is usually called poetic diction; as much pains has been taken to avoid it as is ordinarily taken to produce it; this has been done for the reason already alleged, to bring my language near to the language of men; and further, because the pleasure which I have proposed to myself to impart, is of a kind very different from that which is supposed by many persons to be the proper object of poetry."

This is as direct a challenge to the older generation

as any modern attack upon Victorian standards: and in both cases you notice that the purpose of the revolutionaries is essentially the same. It is to bring poetry down to the level of ordinary common life, to take the starch out of it and put an end to an elaborate specialized "Poetic" diction, which has become a thing apart, a kind of ritual speech, entirely divorced from the easy flow of natural conversation.

But that formal poetry itself, against which Wordsworth was protesting, originated as a similar protest against a too elaborate tradition. We call it for convenience by the general name of "eighteenth-century", since that was the time at which it reached the full height of its glory; but actually we must go a long way further back than the year 1700 before we come to any poetry that is radically different.

Dryden died at the age of sixty-nine in the very year the century was born, but he looks forward to Pope rather than back to Milton. It was with the young Dryden and John Donne and the "school" of poets which Dr. Johnson not inaptly called "Metaphysical" that the Age of Form really and truly began. The schoolboy exuberance of the Elizabethans had given way to the more sober elaboration of Milton, and the time was ripe for a new movement in a different direction.

And what was the idea behind that new literary movement? What was the purpose which inspired the pioneers to break away on a new line? Again let us quote from a contemporary Manifesto:[1] "A constant

[1] *History of the Royal Society*, Thomas Sprat. Statement of the aims of the Royal Society and its intentions towards literature on its foundation in 1662.

Resolution to reject all amplification, digressions, and swellings of style; to return back to the primitive purity and shortness . . . a close, naked, natural way of speaking, positive expressions, clear senses, a native easiness, bringing all things as near the Mathematical plainness as they can, and preferring the language of Artizans, Countrymen, and Merchants before that of Wits and Scholars. . . ." Is not this the same old story—exactly as told by Wordsworth yesterday and by any champion of the new poetry to-day? Poetry, it goes, had got out of hand and run itself into a dead-end: therefore its nose must be turned to point another way, it must be made simple and brought back again into its proper relation with the life of every day.

There is no need to go back any further, in order to see the same thing happening all over again. The truth is, English poetry never has developed in one continuous straight line, but in a series of violent revolts and fresh starts, always in some entirely new direction. A new movement begins, like a thief in the night; almost imperceptibly as—we used to be told in the nursery—bad habits begin. It grows, in the face of opposition, in defiance of the older generation which habitually declares that "this modern poetry may be something else but it certainly isn't Poetry!" Then, as people become accustomed to the new rhythms of speech and novel methods of expression, it challenges the reigning tradition on its own ground: and finally the cry is, "le Roi est mort. Vive le Roi!" But in that triumphant moment the New has become the Old, and it is only a question of time until some fresh upstart movement comes along to dethrone it.

A moralist might find in this a curious resemblance

to the life-process of the average human being. "One man in his time plays many parts"—we remember the melancholy Jaques. He made seven acts of it: but four will suffice for us here. There is first the boy, in his ardent ignorance. He is full of ideas, but without experience to guide him, and the beliefs which his parents hold so sacred he regards with incredulous wonder: ("such outworn platitudes! Things were different when father was young!") And next the adolescent—loud, aggressive because he never feels quite certain of himself, who speaks at the top of his voice in the hope of persuading the world of the importance of what he has to say. Then middle age, the settled prime of a man's life, when a full store of experience is behind him and all his powers lie ready to his hand, disciplined, ordered and controlled. And last the old man, Lear who sees his Kingdom lost, remembering past glories and watching the younger generation going by.

The parallel is both apt and instructive (quite apart from any moral implication). For as a man grows older, you do not expect to find him as supple as he was in his youth. You expect his bones to set more firmly and his muscles to harden. So with poetry. When a new movement begins, all is supple—or, as the tribal elders always will persist in saying, undisciplined and uncontrolled. There is no precedent to put a brake upon experiment. But later when the old tradition has slipped from its throne and is in full retreat, then what once was so new and daring begins to settle into middle age and makes for itself an established tradition of its own, a comprehensive tradition, we may observe, of form and rhythm and diction. Thus there grows up a special kind of language and a special way in which things must be said, which the public ear has become accustomed to regard as "poetical": and poor Poetry finds herself, as time goes on, further and further removed from the carefree unconventional natural speech of men.

. . . .

It is now possible to answer the question, what do we mean by modern poetry? We mean not poetry of this or that particular date, but all the poetry of the new movement from its beginning, the new movement which has broken with the tradition of yesterday and started off on a line of its own. And now we can see what forward-looking means—a revolutionary in fact: "One who never turned his back but marched breast forward," confident that he is swimming in and with the stream of Time.

That there is a new movement and that it started some considerable time ago, everyone is agreed: but you still hear certain fainter-hearted critics plaintively inquiring, "granted all you say, but was it necessary for the Poets to break away so violently? Such a complete reversal, such a turning upside down! Was the Victorian tradition in truth so mouldering and moribund?"

The answer is that after the Victorians came the Georgians: and if you take up any anthology of Georgian Poetry, you find the poets there making exactly that attempt which our faint-hearted critic is recommending by implication. Even before the '90's the hey-day of Victorianism was past, the prime of life, the settled middle-age of that new movement which we saw Wordsworth starting so bravely. A decade and more later, we find the Georgians struggling with their own kaleidoscopic twentieth-century and striving to translate it into terms of a tradition which had become with time as rigid and as tyrannous as Mr. Barrett of Wimpole Street.[1]

There was a convention of words and a convention of rhythm. Poetry is an Art of words. In his chosen medium the poet ought to be as free as Adam and Eve when they left the Garden of Eden:

> the world was all before them, where to choose . . .

But the inheritor of the Victorian tradition was by no means free to choose. Certain words were suitable for poetry, certain others not. Of the latter, as one might expect, a great many were words in common use in "the natural speech of men": not only oaths and epithets, but words indicative of common ordinary things. One might say poetically, for instance:

> Reach down the wedding vesture, that has lain
> Yet all unvisited, the silken gown . . .[2]

but would any Georgian have accepted in a poem this:

> Out of the window perilously spread
> Her drying combinations touched by the sun's last rays
> On the divan are piled (at night her bed)
> Stockings, slippers, camisoles, and stays [3]

I think not; still less any typical Victorian: but Pope would have had no difficulty in recognizing a fellow-craftsman. One other class of words came under the taboo—all those words of comparatively recent origin

[1] My reference is to a purely fictitious character in a purely fictitious work of art: but if it should cause offence, I should be fully prepared to substitute the name of my own grandfather.

[2] *Elegy on a lady, whom grief for the death of her betrothed killed:* Robert Bridges. [3] *The Waste Land*: III, *The Fire Sermon*, T. S. Eliot.

which had been and still were being coined to denote the new things which had been invented and discovered by Science. It must be remembered that the nineteenth century was an age of scientific progress actually unparalleled in the whole of human history: and after the turn of the century Science continued to progress at an equally rapid pace. The steam engine, the petrol engine, the aeroplane, the electric wire, the machine in the factory, the new comfort in the home, completely revolutionized the life of man—at any rate the environmental part of it: and the poetry of the established tradition was at a loss to deal with the results of that revolution. Such strange new words for such strange new things! Words without a pedigree, with no rich store of associations to start trains of ideas in the mind of the reader! One might mention a horse and a carriage, a cow and even a cart—all of them words with a long and respectable family history—but what was to be done with a motor-car? A glamour could be thrown over a church, a house, a hall—even at a pinch a factory (if used adjectivally or carefully hyphenated with another noun)—but what about a gasometer or an electric power station? At all costs poetry must be kept "poetical": with the result that any poet who stuck to the established tradition found himself cut off at least from one half—and that the most important living half—of contemporary life.

And equally insistent and cramping was the convention of rhythm, not merely stereotyped form of metre, but (as Wordsworth said in a different connexion) "something far more deeply interfused". I remember reading an article in some paper or other by Mr. Beverley Nichols. It was in his ever-popular "Garden

Path" vein and entitled, if I remember rightly, "How Grandmamma made a Pot-pourri". It ended on a note of pathos with a reference to the "subtle old-world fragrance which the confection exhaled, reminiscent of the days when Grandmamma herself was young." Just such a fragrance—or rather, since we are dealing with the ear and not the nose, cadence is the better word—just such a cadence haunts all the poetry written in the Victorian tradition. Every poet (early, middle or late) speaks with a touch of the same elusive accent, as indefinable and as clearly recognizable as that of an announcer at the B.B.C. Take any typical example from the great middle period of the century. Take:

> The moony vapour rolling round the king . . .
> Enwound him fold by fold, and made him gray
> And grayer, till himself became as mist
> Before her, moving ghostlike to his doom.

This, of course, is from Tennyson's *Guinevere,* where the high-minded Arthur, after he has expressly told the queen that he forgives her ("as Almighty God forgives"!), refuses to have anything more to do with her in this world and rides off without so much as a good-bye. But it is not the odious priggishness of Arthur's moral outlook that we are considering here: it is the "accent" of Tennyson's verse. Take this passage as a touchstone and apply it anywhere to the Georgian anthology. Take this, for instance:

> Frost, with a gesture, stays the waves that dance
> And wandering loveliness. He leaves a white
> Unbroken glory, a gathered radiance,
> A width, a shining peace, under the night.[1]

[1] *Five Sonnets*: No. IV, *The Dead*, Rupert Brooke (1914).

The two passages are as like as a pair of half-crowns: they have the very same ring upon the counter. Yet the one was minted in the late 'fifties (actually *Guinevere* first appeared in '59), and the other in 1914, on the actual brink of To-day.

There is no need to waste time in multiplying instances: only to notice the effect upon poetry of this Victorian inheritance, which had grown into a veritable Old-man-of-the-sea. What other effect could there be than stultification and a kind of slow strangulation? The same effect that we may perhaps have noticed when a correct and faultless evening dress suit enters the taproom of the local public house. The simplest and friendliest of hearts may beat beneath the boiled shirt front, nevertheless a certain distance and constraint is unavoidable. Once the poets cut themselves off from the full and free speech of their own day, they lost touch automatically with the movement of contemporary life around them. Time moves inexorably on, but they stood still—or rather progressed (if at all) with heads obstinately turned backward: which is not precisely the position most favourable to progress.

Thus poetry once again had come to a parting of the ways. A fresh start at a tangent, a complete reorientation was due and overdue. If it is necessary to hazard a date, the beginning of the new movement, the birth-date of modern poetry, may be placed somewhere between 1909 and 1914. Mr. Michael Roberts in his Introduction to *The Faber Book of Modern Verse* takes 1910. "The poems in this book," he says, "were with few exceptions first printed after 1910. But," he continues, "the date is arbitrary." I take 1909, because when T. S. Eliot published his first collected volume, he dated it *Poems 1909–1925* and it was from him and Ezra Pound that the first authentic notes of the new strain were heard.

But here we are confronted with a paradox. It is true that it was in the years immediately preceding the War, 1914–18, that the voice of the new poetry was first heard. Nevertheless, actually the first poet to break through the Victorian tradition and free both language and metre from the bonds of convention had been dead ten years before the twentieth century opened—but his voice, his very modern voice, had not been heard at all.

CHAPTER II

Gerard Manley Hopkins, Pioneer

GERARD MANLEY HOPKINS was born in 1844: he died in 1889.

These are unexpected dates. They suggest *Sesame and Lilies* and *The Idylls of the King*: beards, ottomans and four-wheel cabs: the palmy days, in fact, of the nineteenth century, the period in which everything that we mean by Victorian came to full flower. The decadence of the '90's had not yet set in, and as for the modern revolt against nineteenth-century standards and "poetical" poetry—the mere idea would have seemed fantastic and incredible. Yet to-day the greatest single influence upon the development of modern poetry, with the solitary exception of T. S. Eliot, has been this stray mid-Victorian—who is anything but mid-Victorian when you come to read him.

This in itself is remarkable: but it is even more remarkable that throughout the '90's, throughout even the nineteen-hundreds when the modern movement in poetry was struggling to make its way, the name of Hopkins should have been entirely unknown. War came in 1914; and in 1916 Robert Bridges published his justly celebrated anthology, *The Spirit of Man*. In it he included six carefully selected little fragments.[1] Meagre though they were and obviously clippings from a bigger file, they were enough to rouse the interest of

[1] *The Spirit of Man*, Robert Bridges, Nos. 9, 53, 269, 358, 369, 385.

the discriminating. Who was this G. M. Hopkins? What had he published? Where could the whole body of his work be found?

Echo answered, where?

Not until 1918, when Dr. Bridges gave to the world the first edition of Hopkins' poems, was the answer given. To that slim little volume he prefixed a graceful sonnet by way of dedication. It opens thus:

> Our generation already is overpast
> And thy lov'd legacy, Gerard, hath lain
> Coy in my home . . .

It is an answer that has been fruitful of controversy. Of Bridges' sincerity there has never been the shadow of a doubt. What he did, he did for the best. The same sonnet continues:

> Dear, the while my hands
> Gather'd thy book, I heard, this wintry day,
> Thy spirit thank me . . .

But was it the best that he did?

At Hopkins' death Bridges became his literary executor—the two had been lifelong friends ever since their first meeting as young men at the University. He found himself left with a bundle of manuscripts which no editor had ever had the courage to print: but their real worth he himself very well knew. For he had seen and criticized them all as they were written, and though they had shocked him not a little, neither his loyalty nor his perception ever wavered. From the first he had no doubt that here was arisen a new poet of quite outstanding originality and power. It was a "lov'd legacy" indeed, but a very awkward one at the same time. The question was, what was the right thing to do with it? "Publish and be damned!" was the Duke of Wellington's advice on a famous occasion, but here the circumstances were hardly the same. It is difficult for us now to realize quite how upsetting, even how monstrous Hopkins' versification would have appeared to the early '90's. What would a generation brought up upon Tennyson's sweet honey and Swinburne's Turkish Delight have made of *Harry Ploughman* [1] or *That Nature is a Heraclitean Fire*? [2] The book must have fallen still-born from the Press or, worse, have been buried under a storm of execration. Bridges would not face either fate for his friend. Better far to wait for the day when the world should be ripe for this new kind of poetry. So he waited—for twenty-eight years.

Whether Bridges did right or wrong will always be a disputed question. That his one thought was how best to serve his friend, no one can doubt. But we may well wonder whether it was not excess of caution to wait until after four years of war the world was prepared to accept practically anything in the way of literary monstrosity: and we may be tempted to imagine what would have been the effect of Hopkins upon the pioneers of the new movement when it was struggling to birth in the days before the War. But all such speculation must be barren. What was done, was done. It is more profitable to turn to Hopkins himself.

There is a portrait of him which stands as frontispiece to the published volume of his letters to Bridges.[3]

[1] *Harry Ploughman*, No. 43, Poems of Gerard Manley Hopkins.

[2] *That Nature is a Heraclitean Fire and of the comfort of the Resurrection*, No. 48, *Ibid.*

[3] *Letters of Gerard Manley Hopkins to Robert Bridges.*

It is a reproduction of a photograph taken when he was nineteen and shows a face singularly delicate and sensitive, with a poet's eye and a scholar's brow. Exactly what you would expect, in fact, of a typical "Portrait of the Artist as a Young Man". What you would not expect (looking at the lower part of the face and the lack of decision in mouth and chin), is to find under the surface a touch of steel. Yet it was there, even when he was a little boy at Highgate School.

There was an occasion on which, having decided that the other boys habitually drank more liquid than was either necessary or good for them, he gave up drinking anything at all, and persisted for a whole week. Naturally the result was a physical collapse and the doctor had to be called in to put the ardent missionary on his legs again. On a later occasion he gave up eating salt for a similar reason. That is one side of him: but there is another, just as clearly marked even in the boy at school and just as unexpected. The portrait in the volume of Letters merely gives an impression of extreme sensitiveness and delicacy of mind: something, in fact, closely resembling the popular conception of Shelley—a kind of disembodied and etherealized angel. But his juvenile verse (and he wrote a great deal) reveals a nature of a very different kind. One quotation will suffice. It comes from a poem written when he was seventeen, which "won a prize for English poetry".

> Plum-purple was the West; but spikes of light
> Spear'd open lustrous gashes, crimson-white . . .
> Anon, across their swimming splendour strook,
> An intense line of throbbing blood-light shook
> A quivering pennon. . . .

No one could claim that these lines are good poetry. They are immature and obviously reminiscent, as schoolboy poetry always must be. Nevertheless, they show very clearly the nature of the writer's mind. Here is no Sensitive Plant such as grew in Shelley's garden, nor

> A poet hidden
> In the light of thought. . . .

On the contrary, it is the world of sensations, the artist's world of feeling, with which he is preoccupied. He is absorbed in it—not in any dilettante way but passionately with his whole being. And primarily, one may notice, it is the light and colour and movement of that world which most attracted him. He sees things with a painter's eye: not with a meditative philosophic eye, like Wordsworth, or architecturally like Hardy, who builds first the huge static background of Nature against which he sets his puppets to play. (It is perhaps significant in this connexion that Hopkins' uncle on his mother's side had some considerable reputation as a landscape painter in his day.) But the point is not so much the direction of this sensuous feeling as its intensity. So strong and so vivid is it and apparently so all-absorbing that you might well believe that this is the whole man: but that is to forget the other and equally forceful side of him, the almost monkish moralist who showed himself so indifferent alike to public opinion and the attractions of the flesh.

The truth is, these two opposites which we see so clearly in the boy are essential elements in the nature of the man: and both his subsequent life and his later poetry are the direct result of the clash and conflict between them.

> I am gall, I am heart-burn: God's most deep decree
> Bitter would have me taste: my taste was me:
> Bones built in me, flesh filled, blood brimmed the curse . . .[1]

Thus he wrote, referring not merely to the opposition of good and evil in him, of the Spirit and the Flesh (that is every man's conflict): but to this further antinomy in his strangely dual nature, in modern jargon, the Will to self-negation perpetually at war with the Will to self-expression.

At nineteen he left school and went up to Balliol College, Oxford, with an exhibition in Classics. Only two events in his University career are worth notice here, but their effect in their different ways upon him could hardly be exaggerated. The one was his meeting with the young Bridges, then like himself an undergraduate in his first year, which resulted in that David and Jonathan friendship between the two poets-to-be which was to end only with Hopkins' death.

The other was his reception in the middle of his last year into the Catholic Church by Cardinal Newman at the Oratory, Birmingham. The boy at school had never done things by halves: nor did the new convert. He wanted immediately to abandon Oxford and all prospect of taking his Final Schools or getting a degree. But Newman, with that wise common sense which always distinguished him, gave better counsel—"Your first duty," he wrote, "is to make a good class. Show your friends that becoming a Catholic has not unsettled you. . . ." So he went back and justified Newman by taking a First Class.

[1] *Poems*, edit. Robert Bridges, 2nd edition, No. 45.

In the autumn of the following year (1868) he entered the Novitiate of the Jesuit Order at Roehampton.

He knew very well what he was doing. The Will to self-negation had triumphed over the Will to self-expression—or in plainer words, the moralist is leading the artist by the nose. "What I had written," he wrote afterwards to Canon Dixon, "I burnt before I became a Jesuit and resolved to write no more, as not belonging to my profession, unless it were by the wish of my superiors; so for seven years I wrote nothing but two or three little presentation pieces which occasion called for. . . ."[1]

Thus outwardly during all those seven years there was silence and submission: but inwardly the new poetry that he was to write was forming and shaping itself, feeling its feet (so to speak) before it had actually come to birth, so that when he does begin to write again the result is something utterly and absolutely different, something in fact quite new and years ahead of its time. It was by a chance (which we may regard as fortunate) that the flood-gates at last were opened. "In the winter of '75," he says later in the same letter, "the *Deutschland* was wrecked in the mouth of the Thames and five Franciscan nuns, exiled from Germany by the Falck laws, aboard of her were drowned. I was affected by the account and happening to say so to my rector he said that he wished someone would write a poem on the subject. On this hint I set to work and, though my hand was out at first, produced one. I had long had haunting my ear the echo of a new rhythm which I now realized on paper. . . ."

What he produced was no "little presentation

[1] *Correspondence of G. M. Hopkins and R. W. Dixon*, Letter III, p. 14.

piece", but a long poem, partly declamatory partly narrative, struck out at white heat and showing in every word and line the intensity of the author's pent-up feeling. He sent it to the *Month*, then, as now, one of the leading Catholic papers which published occasional verse. It is a matter of infinite regret that we have no record of the editor's feelings on glancing for the first time at that remarkable manuscript. "To the happy memory of five Franciscan nuns . . ."—he would have read the sub-title and naturally would expect a set of mild memorial verses or some gentle and pious requiem. Instead he got the *Wreck of the Deutschland*. It must have exploded upon him like a bomb. "Though at first they accepted it," Hopkins tells Canon Dixon, "after a time they withdrew and dared not print it."

One can sympathize with the editor. The year, it must be remembered, was '75. *In Memoriam*, though first published twenty-five years before, was still "for perfection of form and propriety of tone the model for any future elegy". (Compare the first stanza of *The Deutschland* with any section of Tennyson's poem and what worlds we are away!) Even Bridges confessed that "he was himself shamefully worsted in a frontal assault". "The poem," he says in the notes at the end of his edition of Hopkins (*Poems of Gerald Manley Hopkins*, 2nd edition p. 104), "stands logically as well as chronologically in the front of his book, like a great dragon folded in the gate to forbid all entrance. . . . This editor advises the reader to circumvent him and attack him later in the rear."

I cannot help thinking that in thus advising the reader Bridges was wrong. "Logically and chronologically *The Deutschland* stands in the front of his book." It does. The first section of the poem strikes the note, the curious double note, which sounds all through his later poetry and is at once the source of his peculiar power and the clue to his sometimes difficult meaning.

St. 4

I am soft sift
In an hourglass—at the wall
Fast, but mined with a motion, a drift,
And it crowds and it combs to the fall;
I steady as a water in a well . . .
. . . Of the Gospel proffer, a pressure, a principle, Christ's gift.

St. 5

I kiss my hand
To the stars, lovely-asunder
Starlight . . . and
Glow, glory in the thunder;
Kiss my hand to the dappled-with-damson west.

Here is the whole man (or rather the two men in one that together made up the mature poet). You see them set side by side—the ascetic of stanza 4, who for the space of seven years stifled the poet in him for conscience' sake and who could say in a letter which is concerned purely with literary criticism, not with morals, or religion, at all, "the only just judge, the only just literary critic is Christ": and in stanza 5 the other man, the artist, sensuous to his finger-tips, to whom the world of sensation is so intoxicating.

The Wreck of the Deutschland is prelude to his whole work and therefore, I think, not only logically and chronologically but commonsensically one should begin with it.

Admittedly it is not an easy poem. "My hand was out at first," Hopkins said of it himself. Naturally, after so long a silence. In addition, it was his first essay in the new manner: and a new manner in poetry (or in anything else, for that matter), an entirely fresh and original way of saying things, does not spring to birth fully armed and equipped, as did Athene from the brain of Zeus. So on both these counts we should expect *The Deutschland* to be difficult—and it certainly lives up to expectation.

It is divided into two sections of uneven length. The first (and considerably the shorter) is only loosely connected with the second and might quite easily stand as a complete poem by itself. For myself I could wish that it did, though that was by no means Hopkins' own opinion. "*The Deutschland,*" he writes to Bridges (Letter No. XXXIX), "would be more generally interesting if there were more wreck and less discourse, I know, but still it is an ode and not primarily a narrative." The primary motif of the poem is not so much the actual wreck and the drowning of the nuns as the effect of the tragedy upon Hopkins himself: and that is nearly all contained in the first section. In fact, the first section is nothing but a study, as by a flashlight, of his own mind and self at the moment when the poem was written. If it were painted in line and colour instead of in words, it would be labelled "self-portrait by the artist". Everything is there: his hopes, his aspirations, his doubts, his difficulties, his fears, his double self. Was there ever a better description of the life within a religious discipline, "closed by a cassock and dedicate to God"—than this?

St. 2

I did say yes
O at lightning and lashed rod,
Thou heardst me truer than tongue confess
Thy terror, O Christ, O God;
Thou knowest the walls, altar and hour and night:
The swoon of a heart that the sweep and the hurl of thee trod
Hard down with a horror of height:
And the midriff astrain with leaning of, laced with fire of stress.

It is not only the primary motif of *The Deutschland*: it is the constant ground bass to the whole of his poetry, and I agree with Father Lahey in his gentle censure of Bridges, as critic and editor, in that "occasionally he has prescinded" (horrid word!) "from the well-spring of Hopkins' poetry—his religious ideals".[1] Begin then with the "dragon folded in the gate", if only with the first section of him.

The second section is almost wholly narrative: the sailing of the ship from Bremen, the rising storm, the wreck, the heroism and death of the nuns—all set in a fiery nimbus of passionate emotion. The difficulties here are much more in the expression than in the thought. The printed page has a crabbed look. How awkward, for instance, to the eye appears the following:

St. 28

But how shall I . . . make me room there:
Reach me a . . . fancy, come faster—
Strike you the sight of it? look at it loom there,
Thing that she . . . there then! the Master . . .

Even with the context it is hard to make sense of it. But turn to some friend (preferably not one who has taken a course in elocution) and ask him or her to read

[1] *Gerard Manley Hopkins*, G. F. Lahey, S. J., p. 17.

the whole passage aloud—not after the manner of Chaucer's Prioress, who sang

> the servyce dyvyne
> Entuned in hir nose ful semely,

but simply and straightforwardly, with the emphasis falling where instinct naturally dictates. It is astonishing how the crooked will become straight and the rough places plain.

And here we may notice that Hopkins is essentially a poet who wrote to be read aloud. He was well aware how difficult he appears on the printed page and how much of that difficulty vanishes when he is read aloud. "On somebody returning me my Eurydice," he wrote to Bridges in reply to one of the latter's periodic protests, "when I opened and read some lines, as one commonly reads whether prose or verse, with the eyes, so to say, only, it struck me aghast with a kind of raw and unmitigated violence I was unprepared for: but take breath and read it with the ears, as I always wish to be read, and my verse becomes all right." The difference is almost miraculous. It is not only that often what seems in print impossibly crude and difficult will sound entirely natural and simple when the ear alone is judge: but the voice brings out so much more than the mere sense of the words. For Hopkins was always a most careful and painstaking craftsman. A host of little subtleties springs suddenly to light, which in the printed page might and often do remain completely unsuspected. I mean such devices as deliberate and sometimes concealed Assonance (as in the sonnet, No. 45 in *Poems*, 2nd edition):

> O what black hours we have spent
> This night! What sights you, heart, saw . . .

and his frequent use of Alliteration and Interior Rhymes.

The originality of Hopkins' method in *The Deutschland* and in everything that he wrote subsequently is twofold. He uses a rhythm the like of which had never before fallen upon staid Victorian ears: and he treats words (and grammar too) with a freedom that made Bridges wince and is sometimes too much for us even now. For example, in the closing line of that otherwise magnificent sonnet (No. 44 in *Poems*, 2nd edition) he writes:

> Heard unheeded, leaves me a lonely began.

You may take your choice whether he intended to leave out both relative and antecedent before that very odd final word "began", meaning "leaves me a lonely man who has only just begun", or flatly to use the past tense of a verb as a noun.

But is this not exactly the same revolt from Victorian tradition which "modern" poetry has made within recent years? Is it not exactly that same first step which we saw in the preceding chapter poetry had to take, if she were to save her soul alive—a complete and violent break with orthodox rhythm and orthodox diction?

"I had long had haunting my ear the echo of a new rhythm . . . 'Sprung' Rhythm, as I call it." What was this new rhythm with so odd and uninformative a name?

> I caught this morning morning's minion, king-
> dom of daylight's dauphin, dapple-dawn-drawn Fal-
> con, in his riding
> Of the rolling level-underneath-him steady air, and striding ..

Thus begins *The Windhover* (*Poems*, 2nd edition, No. 12). It is a sonnet of the correct length of fourteen lines (a fact which if not immediately obvious to the eye may be discovered by counting): and the rhyming correctly follows a fixed scheme. But how shall it be scanned?

We might start with the usual method (what Hopkins in his Author's Preface calls "the common rhythm in English use"), division into feet of so many syllables each. Thus at a pinch the first line might be an ordinary five-foot iambic, like the beginning of any familiar sonnet: for example,

Avenge / O Lord / thy slaught / ered saints, / whose bones . . .

But the second refuses absolutely to be so treated. It has too many words: it is too bulky. We may well scratch our heads and ask

> Upon what meat doth this our Cæsar feed
> That he is grown so great?

And out of Hopkins' mouth we take the answer—upon this mysterious Sprung Rhythm. There is nothing mysterious about what he meant. He meant a rhythm in which one does not count by syllables but by stresses (a stress being either one word or a group of words upon which the emphasis of the voice falls). So many stresses go to make one line: and it does not matter in the least, provided the requisite stresses are all present and correct, how long or short the line may be. Any number of unemphasized syllables may cluster round each separate stress—on the ancient principle, if one may be so vulgar, that "big fleas have little fleas . . .", the total sum for purposes of enumeration being One Flea.

The rhythm is a rhythm of stress. Why then call it "Sprung"? The name was Hopkins' own invention and very proud he was of it, as one may fairly infer from his letters: but I cannot think it a particularly happy choice. "Sprung," according to the dictionary, means either "furnished with springs" or exactly the opposite. "All my beds are sprung," says the landlady hopefully, and the new lodger after a night upon the rack finds out for himself the truth of her description. What connexion has either of these meanings with scansion by stress? Only this perhaps—that a line scanned solely by stress may be thought of as running on springs and each individual stress may by a further effort of imagination be likened to a single spring which may consist of any number of coils. Hopkins himself might have given a fuller and more convincing explanation, but it is not on record that he ever did.

"Sprung" rhythm itself, of course, was by no means a new discovery. Actually it is the oldest rhythmic principle in our tongue. What was new was Hopkins' adaptation and amplification of it. It is the rhythm of nursery rhyme and the popular jingle: of

> The queen was in her parlour
> Eating bread and honey.

and of

> O Mr. Porter,
> Whatever shall I do?
> I want to go to Birmingham
> And they've put me down at Crewe!

It was the rhythm of all Old English verse; and it was the rhythm in which at the close of the fourteenth century Langland (if that really was his name!) wrote his *Piers Plowman*. After that it scarcely ever appears as a vehicle for serious poetry. The other principle, of counting by syllables and regular feet, had already begun to make its way across the Channel: and behind it was all the prestige of cultured France and Renaissance Italy. Naturally therefore, like Julius Cæsar, it came and saw and conquered. Chaucer was Langland's almost exact contemporary, but, unlike that gentle visionary, he was a " modern " of his period and at the same time a poet of the very first rank. He took the new prosody—really it was nothing but the old prosody of ancient Greece and Rome, which everyone who has studied Greek and Latin verse at school knows so well—and showed that what had been done with it in other languages could be done with it in English too. Our native rhythm consequently suffered a " loss of face ", from which it never recovered for the space of six centuries. Then at long last a Jesuit priest, in revolt against contemporary sophistication, demonstrated to an unbelieving generation that a writer of genius could produce great poetry in the old rhythm of stress, just as well as in any other.

But Hopkins did not stop short at rhythmic innovation. Even more revolutionary is his treatment of language, his whole attitude in fact towards everything that is contained between the covers of a grammar book. It is not only that he is never a slave to precedent. It is more than that. He uses words with all the fine careless rapture of Browning's famous thrush: and when it suits him, he can be as indifferent to the niceties of grammatical construction as Jones Minor of the Lower Fourth.

Turn again to *The Windhover*:

> . . . dapple-dawn-drawn Falcon, in his riding
> Of the rolling level-underneath-him steady air . . .

How fresh and how complete is the picture which these odd-looking compound epithets evoke! At the same time a large part of that freshness is due to their oddness: for they are monsters unknown to any dictionary, being compounded according neither to precedent nor principle, save only the instinct of a genuine and original poet. Or look further, to the first and second lines of the sextet:

> Brute beauty and valour and act, oh, air, pride, plume, here
> Buckle!

What meaning shall we give to " buckle "? What it must mean is unmistakable. He sees a kestrel in flight: and beauty and daring and mastery, the " rolling level-underneath-him " air, the arrogant look of the bird as he flies, the feathered wings that bear him so buoyantly—all these are elements (they " meet together ") in that moment's vision. But " buckle "! Search for authority or even shadow of a precedent and you will find none. The word ought not to bear such a meaning. Nevertheless when you read it in its context, it not only must, but does!

Or turn from *The Windhover* and look at another and very typical flat defiance of orthodoxy. " The omission of the relative," Bridges protests in the Preface to his Notes, " though it is a common convenience in conversation . . . is apt to confuse the parts of speech and to reduce a normal sequence of words to a mere jargon ": and he cites as an example the prayer in *The Loss of the Eurydice* (*Poems*, 2nd edition, No. 17, 111–112).

> Holiest, loveliest, bravest
> Save my hero, O Hero savest.

Seeing this for the first time in print, I think, the eye must inevitably confuse the mind. But listen to it with the ear alone and I very much doubt whether anyone, even a stalwart of the old school, would have more than a momentary hesitation as to what the second line is intended to mean. And certainly, once it is realized that " O Hero savest " means " O Hero who savest ", that is " Christ, our Saviour ", one can never be in doubt again.[1]

There is more point in Bridges' second example, which he takes from the almost-but-never-quite successful *Bugler's First Communion* (*Poems*, 2nd edition, No. 23). The young soldier is kneeling at the altar-rail and the priest administering the Sacrament prays over him:

> Frowning and forefending angel-warder
> Squander the hell-rook ranks sally to molest him.

Here neither to the eye nor ear is the grammatical construction of the second line immediately obvious. It is not even obvious that both " squander " and " sally " are meant to be verbs. One has to take thought: and the only indication that a relative has been omitted before the latter of the two words is the reflection that the priest could hardly have been pronouncing a Satanist blessing and calling on the hell-

[1] Vide *Letters of G. M. Hopkins to Robert Bridges*, Letter LIX, in which Hopkins rebukes him for his " unaccountable misunderstanding " of these two lines.

rooks to sally to molest his protégé! But you cannot expect a pioneer, even a pioneer of genius, to hit the centre of the target every time. Hopkins' failures are conspicuous, as every failure must be that comes from strength and not from weakness. He can write:

> And leaves me a lonely began.

But he can also write:

> That night, that year
> Of now done darkness I wretch lay wrestling with (my God!) my God.

There is no parallel to that kind of writing anywhere in the nineteenth century: nor in the eighteenth: nor in Donne, even in his most magnificent moments: nor yet in Milton. Not until you go back to Shakespeare himself do you find another bold and original genius who regards words in the light of that celebrated precept—" the Sabbath was made for man, not man for the Sabbath ".

" But me no buts," says Shakespeare, boldly making both a noun and a verb out of what a grammarian would insist was a simple little conjunction. Exactly similar is Hopkins' adjective-into-verb translation in *Carrion Comfort* (*Poems*, 2nd edition, No. 40):

> But ah, but O thou terrible, why dost thou rude on me
> Thy wring-world right foot rock?

And as for " level-underneath-him steady air " (which we have already quoted from *The Windhover*), did not Shakespeare write in Sonnet, No. 57:

> Nor dare I chide the world-without-end hour? [1]

[1] One of a series of parallels quoted by Dr. Leavis in *New Bearings in English Poetry* in convincing refutation of the opinion expressed by the editor of the 2nd edition of the poems, that " Hopkins' true affinity is with Milton, not with Shakespeare ".

The two bold and masterful compound epithets are own brothers. In his hands the English language became fluid once again, as it had never been since Elizabethan times. And it is just this Shakespearean independence and refusal to be bound by authority or custom that makes him (historically) the first of the moderns.

CHAPTER III

The New Movement—Imagism—New Ideas and New Language

ALL new literary movements have a similar origin and start with a similar aim. Like the New Year resolutions which one makes and in due course breaks, they originate in dissatisfaction with the past and aim at "turning over a new leaf"—which in the case of Poetry means an attempt to return to the method and manner of ordinary natural speech. But there all similarity ends. No two movements could be expected to develop in precisely the same way, since all Poetry, so long as it remains alive and vital, must be in touch with the life of its own day. In fact, the general characteristics of any "period" will be reflected in the poetry which is written in it. The Elizabethan poets, for instance, mirror (it is Shakespeare's word) life as it was in Elizabethan times, vigorous, exuberant, tender and violent, child-like and worldly-wise. And are not the Victorians (broadly speaking) —Victorian? Consider the general characteristics of that period: grave in the old Roman sense of "gravitas", serious (we remember Matthew Arnold on the "high seriousness of great poetry"), sentimental rather than tender, placidly certain that their way was the Only Way. And Modern Poetry is—but we must look to the modern world for an answer, or at least a large part of the answer.

The Victorian world broke up in a shower of pieces, each piece a belief once cherished, a "truth" once considered unshakable. Science was the villain. New inventions and (what is more important) new ideas which were the cause of the new inventions came crowding so thick that men's minds could not move fast enough to cope with them. Mentally the average man requires time to adjust himself to conditions which are entirely novel. The activities of science gave him no time at all. The result was a natural bewilderment, accompanied (as so often happens under similar conditions, on the ancient principle "omne ignotum pro magnifico") by a wave of enthusiasm for the new knowledge that could achieve such marvels. Even the charmed circles of orthodox religion and academic learning, which ever since the time of Roger Bacon had been implacably hostile to every kind of experimental investigation, were forced, so to speak, to sit up and take notice. For Bergson and Bertrand Russell had superseded Kant and Hegel, and (what is more) achieved a considerable measure of popularity outside the ranks of the pure intellectuals. Schools began to take the teaching of science seriously, no longer treating it as a poor relation who receives the charity of an attic bedroom, but as a subject of equal status even with the time-honoured "Classics". And this meant that there issued from the schools an increasing number of young people trained if not in the elements, at any rate in the methods of science. They looked out upon the world (as they had been taught to do) with bright, enthusiastic eyes, like the eyes of a bird looking for the early morning worm: probing here, testing there, but caring nothing for what Authority might have said in the past, unless it should be found to square with the result of their own observations in the present. And this general scepticism, of course, included a critical estimate of the older generation. A cry went up from innumerable elderly bosoms: "This growing irreverence of the young! Whatever is the country coming to?"

The country was coming to a rising generation whose outlook was scientific, rather than romantic or purely intellectual or purely moral. And how could reverence be expected of such a generation, since irreverence is the key-note of the scientific method? "Doubt all," said the philosopher Descartes, "for only after doubt can knowledge come!" That is the way of science. "Examine all, put everything to the only valid test of truth, Experience. Always be prepared to find that fresh experience may contradict the truth which experience has already shown. . . ."

It was a world of scepticism and inquiry with which the poets had to deal, a world much more inclined to look forward with excitement to new things in the future than backwards to the achievements of the past. The Georgians tried to reflect it in their poetry (when they were not deliberately trying to escape from it). They failed—except in certain isolated instances—as they were bound to fail, because they would persist in using a language that had become hopelessly out of date and consequently put themselves at one remove from the actualities of their own time.

There followed (or, rather, there intervened) a curious little movement which bestowed on itself the imposing name of "Imagism". It began some six years or so before the War and finally expired with the publication of its last collected volume, *Some Imagist Poets,* in 1917. Imagism was a revolt against Georgian ineffectiveness, and at first sight might seem the real beginning of Modern Poetry, the first step towards twentieth-century emancipation. And in a sense, it was. You find, for instance,[1] the founder and chief spokesman of the Imagists writing thus: "I object even to the best of the Romantics . . . I object to the sloppiness which doesn't consider that a poem is a poem unless it is moaning or whining about something or other. The thing has got so bad now that a poem which is dry and hard, a properly classical poem, would not be considered poetry at all. How many people can lay their hands on their hearts and say they like either Horace or Pope?" Every word of this can be exactly paralleled in the *Critical Essays* of T. S. Eliot.

But this was only the negative half of the Imagist creed. The other, the positive and operative half was so deliberately self-limiting and could so obviously lead only into a cul-de-sac that one wonders how anyone of sensibility and intelligence could ever have seriously adopted it. It was based ultimately (though not directly) upon a celebrated *jeu d'esprit*, which was loosed upon the world by Edgar Allan Poe in an essay upon *The Poetic Principle*. In it he argues with all the plausibility which always attaches to an undeniable half-truth that "the degree of excitement which would entitle a poem to be so called at all cannot be sustained throughout a composition of any great length." This, in effect, became Article I of the Imagist creed. Poe had merely asserted that Poetry appears only in flashes and that a poem of any length must consist of long tracts of prosaic desert enlivened

[1] *Speculations*, E. T. Hulme.

by a rare oasis here and there. The Imagists rejected everything but the short poem. Hence their self-chosen name. A poem must be to the reader's mind what an image is to the retina of the eye at any given moment of perception. It is an affair of a moment: yet everything that the eye sees is present and comprehended in it. "A poem is an image or a succession of images, and an image is that which presents an intellectual or emotional complex in an instant of time."

Logically, therefore, we may observe, the ideal poem would consist of a single word, supposing you could find one which would fulfil the necessary condition of suggesting both the subject of the poem and the whole range of associations which the mind connects with it. I can myself think off-hand of two quite simple words. Monosyllables, of course (to conform to the Imagist doctrine, "the shorter the better"). Either would fulfil both parts of the required condition, striking upon the ear like an arresting clap of thunder and rolling away into an infinity of reverberate associations; but actually no Imagist poem that has achieved the dignity of print is of less than two lines' length.

Starting then with this obsession of cameo-size and a further limitation as to the kind of subject it was permissible to choose, (it must be something, like a visual image, hard, clear-cut and concrete), the Imagist had to contrive some method of making his projected poem into a poem. But how? The ordinary method, of drawing out the ideas inherent in the subject and allowing the poet's imagination to play upon them, clashed with the theory that an image is "that which presents an intellectual and emotional complex in an instant of time". It was moreover the method of the

Georgians, against whose whole conception of poetry Imagism was a deliberate and conscious protest: and of the Victorians before them. Even the eighteenth century, the Age of "properly classical poetry", had had an unfortunate habit of writing at length. Where then was the new revolutionary movement to turn? For somewhere a source of inspiration had to be found. No literary movement ever can or ever did start straight into the blue, without any affinities or associations with what has gone before. Absolute originality, in this sense, is an absolute myth.

There was no help to be had from any of the English poets from Tennyson to Chaucer, but there was a fully fledged "modernist" movement in France, which dated back to the '90's, and ultimately derived, like Imagism itself, from the æsthetic of Edgar Allan Poe. This was the movement known as Symbolism, a name that has now become almost as familiar as a topic of pseudo-intellectual conversation as the doctrines of Dr. Freud. The Imagists turned to it as the Israelites turned to their manna: but they selected from Symbolist practice only such parts as suited their own particular theories.

Symbolism really, in the last analysis, was nothing more than an extension (though a very considerable extension) of the ancient principle that poetry makes its effect very largely by means of suggestion. Direct statement would often be too long and at times quite inadequate to express everything that the poet has in mind to say. Therefore he must choose his words not alone for reasons of fitness or harmony, but to stand, if need be, for more than themselves and rouse a flock of associations in the mind of the reader, like a voice echoing round a whispering gallery. And this may be extended to groups of words and phrases—even to whole sentences. I happen to remember (as one does remember snatches of the things one learnt with pain and labour at school), four lines of Longfellow, from a set of not very distinguished verses called *Resignation*. "Sunt lacrimae rerum" is his theme (in the immortal phrase of a far greater poet).

> The air is full of farewells to the dying
> And mournings for the dead;
> The heart of Rachel for her children crying
> Will not be comforted.

Here the third and fourth lines of the quatrain mean something quite other (or rather something far more extensive) than what they actually say. The poet means, of course, that in his own day there were many mothers in the world mourning for the loss of their children as bitterly as Rachel once mourned for the loss of hers. He does not say so: he short-circuits, and thereby says much more. The reference to Rachel instantly recalls her story as told in the Bible and all the emotions connected with it in our minds: and further, the poet (without a word said) has linked the sorrows of the present with the sorrows of the past. And this is not only an instance of poetry's working by suggestion. It is also a perfect example of what the Symbolists meant by a "symbol".

And what did they mean? Coleridge, in one of his looser moments, once declared that there were certain poems which he would prefer to read without trying to understand the whole of what they meant. Poe took this up (as he took many of Coleridge's ideas) and elaborated it into a theory. "Music," he said, must be an essential element in all true poetry: and by "music" he meant not simply lilt or cadence, as one might expect, but the indefiniteness which is inherent in the use of pure sound as a medium of expression. Words have a definite meaning: musical notes have not. Was it possible for poetry to imitate the vague indefinite effects that music can achieve? The Symbolists answered, yes: and they went further. It was not only possible but necessary in certain cases. For there are emotions and feelings common to all of us which are so infinitely subtle as to defy a definite analysis. Supposing the poet never spoke his direct thought but only hinted at it? Supposing he took certain things and used them each to suggest a whole range of other things? The possibilities were infinite. "My aim," said Mallarmé, theorizing about his own poetry, "is to evoke an object in deliberate shadow, without ever actually mentioning it, by allusive words, never by direct words."

All this of course was entirely foreign to Imagist ideas. They were not concerned with the evocation of subtleties too intricate or too elusive for plain straightforward statement: nor were they trying to reproduce in words the infinitely various cross-currents and complexities of modern life. Their aim was to abolish Georgian prolixity and make poetry direct, short and simple, or (as they themselves put it) to present a clear-cut concrete image which should be as complete as possible and yet contained within the smallest possible compass. But this meant that they too, like the Symbolists (though for very different reasons), were obliged to short-circuit; and there ready to their hands was the Symbolist method of association and suggestion. A most accommodating Vicar-of-Bray-like method, we may notice. Originally designed to produce an effect of vague indefiniteness, in Imagist hands it becomes an instrument for packing the maximum of definite meaning into the minimum of available space.

Imagism, as a movement and as a force, is very thoroughly dead. Nevertheless it was in its day the prelude to modern poetry and serves us now as a kind of preparatory course before we approach the real thing. To give the Imagists their due, they were the first to make a complete revolt, lock, stock and barrel, against the Victorian and Georgian tradition. They saw that the nineteenth-century world had acquired a new point of view and that without a new point of view poetry must remain out of touch and sympathy with the age. They went abroad for their ideas: they succeeded in introducing the rather ladylike and insular English Muse to the revolutionary theories of the Symbolists across the water—an introduction which has led to a liaison that seems, at any rate at the present moment, quite likely to be permanent. Finally (and for this we may be truly thankful) not all those who started the movement with enthusiasm remained in it to the end. They saw too clearly what that end must be. Poetry (to be any good at all) must progress, either at a tangent or in a straight line: but Imagism had made itself a closed circle. Therefore the bolder and more vital spirits passed on, whilst the others, having ordered their own little coffin, deliberately shut themselves up in it and perished.

Two quotations will suffice to show what Imagism

at its best could achieve: also, what it could not, in consequence of the severe and arbitrary restrictions which it had imposed upon itself. We may take this, as an example of "the intellectual and emotional complex compressed into an instant of time":

O Fan of white silk,
    Clear as frost on the grass-blade,
You also are laid aside.[1]

And this, slightly longer but still conforming strictly to Imagist theory:

Whirl up sea,
Whirl your pointed pines.
Splash your great pines
On our rocks.
Hurl your green over us—
Cover us with your pools of fir.[2]

The actual "image", and what is suggested to the mind by the image, are all there, packed into the smallest possible space; but brevity is achieved at a price.

We may now return from this somewhat lengthy digression to the point from which we started. What effects had the changed conditions of this twentieth-century world upon the face and form of poetry? We might answer with perfect truth: "effects as many and as various as modern life itself—far too many to be discussed at the length of a single chapter": but there are two in particular which are outstanding and must strike even the most casual reader at first glance. The change wrought by science was far-reaching and comprehensive. It altered for an overwhelming majority

[1] *Lustra*, Ezra Pound, "Fan-piece, For Her Imperial Lord".
[2] *The Oread*, H. D.

of people both their way of thinking and their way of living. " I look around me and what do I see? The grand old Classical Tradition falling into desuetude; our young people sent forth from school trained to look out upon God's fair world as through the windows of a scientist's laboratory; a general Scepticism everywhere replacing a general Reverence; in our mouths and nostrils the pernicious intoxicant of Free Thought and Disbelief, so that well may we exclaim with Tennyson's Tithonus, 'And all I was, in ashes!'"[1] This is perhaps a little on the emotional side: but if you discount that and its obvious reactionary bias, it comes very near to the truth.

And was it possible for a new movement, professedly aiming at what Kipling called the " common touch ", to shut its eyes to this new aspect of modern life which was becoming more important and insistent day by day? It was a field that was almost virgin. For Science, according to Victorian ideas, as a subject for Poetry, had been almost completely taboo. Poetry must be "poetical" (in the bad old sense of that really impossible word): but all these new things—the inventions of science and scientific processes and scientific terminology—were exactly the reverse. They were "practical". They were too new to have acquired even a suspicion of glamour. Consequently if a poet touched them at all, he must do so with the utmost circumspection. Think, for instance, of Tennyson's difficulties in the " Princess ":

> A dozen angry models jetted steam:
> A petty railway ran: a fire-balloon

[1] I take this from the correspondence column of a daily paper of the year 1908.

Rose gem-like up before the dusky groves
And dropt a fairy parachute and past:
And there thro' twenty posts of telegraph
They flashed a saucy message to and fro
Between the mimic stations; so that sport
Went hand in hand with Science . . .

It has a monstrous archness. Subject and expression are not fused and interfused. They go uneasily together. But turn to a modern poet, who accepts all the component parts of modern life as natural and therefore stuff out of which poetry is to be made:

After the first powerful plain manifesto
The black statement of pistons, without more fuss
But gliding like a queen, she leaves the station.
. . . .
Beyond the town there lies the open country
Where, gathering speed, she acquires mystery,
The luminous self-possession of ships on ocean.
It is now she begins to sing—at first quite low
Then loud, and at last with a jazzy madness—
The song of her whistle screaming at curves,
Of deafening tunnels, brakes, innumerable bolts,
And always light, aerial, underneath
Goes the elate metre of her wheels.[1]

Here all the material, the awkward facts, the embarrassing new things of the new world, have been unconditionally accepted and absorbed. And therefore it comes out a homogeneous whole, naturally and inevitably transmuted into poetry.

Thus do we think differently to-day: and as for our living differently—the measure of the change is the growth of our industrial towns, our Manchesters and our Birminghams. We are to-day preponderantly an

[1] *Poems*, Stephen Spender XXXII, *The Express*.

urban people. A great and still growing majority, as it was bred in the town and spends most of its life there, thinks in terms of the town. And this, of course, has had its effect upon poetry. No longer will you expect to find the poets drawing their metaphors solely or even primarily from Nature and the age-old traditional life of the countryside. They too think largely in terms of the town: and urban similes come as naturally to their lips as rural conceits to the writers of Elizabethan Pastoral.

The first really satisfying product of the modern movement—a genuine poem worthy of the name, as opposed to a *tour-de-force*, a *jeu d'esprit* not in the best of taste, a naughty experiment, the mindless rakings of the contemporary muck-keep (to adopt the language with which the New Poetry was received by the critics of the day)—was T. S. Eliot's *Love-song of J. Alfred Prufrock*. This originally appeared in 1914 in Ezra Pound's *Catholic Anthology* of modernist verse, to be greeted by a chorus the reverse of approving. Nowadays we think differently of it and would be prepared to go almost as far as Mrs. Monro, who says of it in her introduction to *Recent Poetry* that "the influence of Prufrock upon the poetry of our time has been almost as disturbing as the murder at Sarajevo was to the peace of Europe".

It begins uncompromisingly in the new manner thus:

> Let us go then, you and I,
> When the evening is spread out against the sky
> Like a patient etherised upon a table.

When one read this for the first time, it seemed (excusably perhaps) nothing more than the effort of a young man trying to be clever, racking his brains to find a comparison sufficiently exotic to shock the unoffending reader. But really it is not exotic at all.[1] The poem deals with a little drama that might have its setting in any town—the abortive attempt at self-expression of a mildly amorous gentleman of middle age over the tea-cups. A winter's evening is drawing on: and the poet, looking for a simile, naturally turns not to anything rustic or invested with the glamour of a poetic past, but to the ordinary twentieth-century familiar life of the town. He can be quite confident that whatever he may choose of that kind will be equally familiar to his readers. Their outlook is urban. They will understand.

[1] Though it may be and is deliberately reminiscent—both image and idea being taken from the Symbolist poet, Jules Laforgue: "from the study of whom" (as Eliot himself says) "the form in which I began to write was directly drawn".

I am indebted to Miss A. E. Mackay for pointing this out to me.

CHAPTER IV

The War, 1914-1918, and its Poetry

MODERN Poetry, as it happened, chose a very awkward moment to be born. Ten, or even five, years earlier who knows what the difference might have been? If only Gerard Hopkins had been known and not left lying in lavender in Bridges' bottom drawer! But as it was, no sooner had the modern infant found its feet and uttered one loud intelligible cry [1] than there came the 1914–18 War.

The War threw back poetry at least thirty years—if not right back into the arms of her old Victorian grandmother, who might be moribund but was by no means finally deceased. A fundamental certainty had been the distinctive mark of the circles in which grandmother moved. All that, like the shades of night in Haydn's *Creation,* had gradually vanished before the radiant beams of the New Knowledge. But now with the outbreak of war that same certainty returned. Doubts melted: once again men could passionately believe. Indeed they had to, for their own peace of mind. For a nation going to war always passionately believes in two things at any rate—the essential justice of its own cause and that God is on the side of the Right. Otherwise there would be no war.

The new poetry had been trying to find (and in *Prufrock* had actually succeeded in finding) a way to

[1] That loud cry, of course, was *Prufrock*, first unmistakable sign that the child was neither cretinous nor abortive and would one day grow into a man.

express the complexities of the modern world and the perplexities of modern life in language which should be at once natural and flexible. But suddenly on that fateful 4th August, 1914, all those complexities narrowed down into one overwhelming simplicity. *Malbrouck s'en va-t-en guerre.* That old cry filled everyone's heart and mind. Your King and Country need you.

It was a simple emotion. Neither complexity nor perplexity had any place in it: nothing but a settled conviction, a Victorian certainty that there was only one Right Thing to do. There were, of course, individuals here and there who had an opposite kind of certainty or who had no such certainty at all—but they were never very many. The vast majority of the nation was filled with patriot fervour to the exclusion of all else. Even those who had immediately ensconced themselves in soft jobs at home were entirely convinced that it was the other fellow's bounden duty to go out and fight.

> By all the glories of the day
> And the cool evening's benison,
> By that last sunset touch that lay
> Upon the hills when day was done,
> . . . .
> Make me a soldier, Lord.[1]

It was also an emotion that had endless precedent: and precedent makes glamour.

> Sleep not, my country, though night is here, afar
> Your children of the morning are clamorous for war:
> Fire in the night, O dreams!
> Though she send you as she sent you long ago,
> South to desert, East to ocean, West to snow . . .

[1] *Before Action*, William Noel Hodgson, *Poems of To-day*, 2nd Series, No. 3.
[2] *The Dying Patriot*, J. E. Flecker.

Not England alone, but every nation at some time or another had sent her sons. . . . Naturally therefore the poets turned back to the past. Glamour and the crisis of the moment working together heightened their mood to the point of exaltation. They looked back over history. Even so must all Greece have been stirred when the Spartan Old Contemptibles marched to hold the pass at Thermopylæ: and even so the city of Rome, when her war-worn eagles crossed the hills to meet Hannibal on the plain of Cannæ. Surely this was no common or ordinary emotion! How then should it be expressed in common or ordinary language, the natural speech of the man in the street, which was apparently the aim and ideal of the new poetry?

You find in the poetry of the early days of the War a return to Victorian tradition, both in language and in rhythm. The War gave the poets no time to think things out. War never does: it stimulates feeling, but never thought. Even a philosopher, if you throw a bucket of water over him, has no time at the moment to philosophize, but he feels intensely. So the poets, passionately desiring to give immediate and adequate expression to the emotions which were surging inside them, turned back to a tradition which had not yet wholly lost its glamour.

The result is that none of that poetry, even the best of it, is entirely convincing. Over and above the reversion to the old rhythms and the old "poetical" language that was so far removed from the common speech of the day, you cannot help feeling that the whole man is never fully behind the poem. The poets write out of that part of themselves which was filled with martial ardour: all the rest is in abeyance. But poetry, to be fully satisfying, must be completely and absolutely sincere. A great poem may represent a mood only, a fancy, a fragment of the writer's full thought, nevertheless you feel that his whole personality has gone to the making of it. It can never be partial, in the sense that it is false to any essential part of the poet's real self.

But that fullness, that complete sincerity, is exactly what is missing in the early poetry of the War. Can anyone, for instance, believe that the whole mind of Hardy was engaged when he wrote the Song of the Soldiers, *Men who march away*?

> In our heart of hearts believing
> Victory crowns the just
> And that braggarts must
> Surely bite the dust . . .

Set the satisfied and complacent certainty of this beside *In Time of the Breaking of Nations* (which comes only three or four pages later in the same volume, *Poems of War and Patriotism*): or beside that final paragraph which is epilogue to his Durberville epic—"'Justice' was done, and the President of the Immortals had ended his sport with Tess . . .". In which speaks the whole man?

Or take even those five sonnets, *1914*, on which Rupert Brooke's reputation chiefly rests. That reputation is somewhat diminished now. (One wonders how much of it was due to the fortuitous conjunction of great personal good looks and an honourable and untimely death.)

> Now, God be thanked who has matched us with His hour,
> And caught our youth, and wakened us from sleeping,

With hand made sure, clear eye, and sharpened power,
  To turn, as swimmers into cleanness leaping,
Glad from a world grown old and cold and weary

. . . .

Oh! we, who have known shame, we have found release there,
  Where there's no ill, no grief, but sleep has mending,
  Naught broken save this body, lost but breath;
Nothing to shake the laughing heart's long peace there
  But only agony, and that has ending;
    And the worst friend and enemy is but Death.

When I read these sonnets, I always think of our local amateur theatricals and Mr. Gass, the chemist, playing the Pirate King. Valiantly he acts the part, desperately he tries to convince us that he actually is that superman of blood and thunder: and, being an actor of quite unusual skill for an amateur, almost he persuades me. But I know that the real Mr. Gass is something very different, both greater (because more human) and less (because less picturesque) than his impersonation.

The fact is, the poets in 1914 were turning themselves into soldiers, either in act or in intention: but by no means all the qualities that go to make a proper man are either needed or desired in a proper soldier. If you can manage to read, with attention and imagination, the *Manual of Infantry Training* (edition of any date) or its more ferocious companion *Instructions in Bayonet Fighting*, you will gather just how much—or just how little—is required of the ideal military man. You must read between the lines, of course: for the Authorities have stopped short at including a character-sketch in plain unequivocal words.

And what out of the whole range of qualities that go to make a man's full nature are those which are useful in a soldier? They may be counted on the hand.

There is courage—that of course goes without saying: and there is endurance—"they stood, and Earth's Foundations stay": and there is Obedience—this with a capital O, since in some ways it is the most important of all—"theirs not to reason why, theirs but to do and die": and lastly there is pugnacity—which means, if you read your manuals carefully, a healthy hate of the designated enemy. Anything beyond these is either unnecessary (and therefore better not in evidence) or likely actually to impair efficiency. This then was the straw out of which in those early days the poets made their bricks—working under an urgent taskmaster who allowed them no time in which to pause and reflect or (to use Milton's phrase) "strictly meditate the thankless Muse".

But the War protracted itself. The hopeful prospect of a speedy victory for Justice and the Right grew more and more remote. And further, it ceased to be a war of movement, which might have kept alive for a considerable period the first spontaneous excitement and enthusiasm: instead, the War became static, frozen into an immobility which seemed likely to last indefinitely. The armies sat down *vis-à-vis* in trenches; and there began that nightmare travesty of a life fit for reasonable beings, so ironically reminiscent at moments of the daily round, the common task of peaceful life at home. It was, in army parlance, certainly no tea-party: but since the alarums and excursions were not entirely continuous, it did at least give the civilian-turned-soldier a little more time to think. Gradually those other elements in his human nature, which had been submerged in the first flush of martial ardour ("Make me a soldier, Lord"), began to raise their diminished heads. Men's thoughts began to turn from the all-absorbing unifying Cause to the separate individual entities who were bearing the burden of the Cause. Consequently you find a change in the poetry of the War which becomes more and more marked as time goes on.

You may see this very clearly, if you take the second volume of that designedly "un-modern" anthology, *Poems of To-day*. It opens with a poem by Robert Nichols in the typical beginning-of-the-War tradition. The last verse contains the kernel:

> O bronzen pines, evening of gold and blue,
> Steep mellow slope, brimmed twilit pools below,
> Hushed trees, still vale dissolving in the dew,
> Farewell! Farewell! There is no more to do.
> We have been happy. Happy now I go.[1]

But now turn six pages on. Again a war-poem by the same writer, but how changed the emphasis, how different the outlook!

> Faces cheerful, full of whimsical mirth,
> Lined by the wind, burned by the sun;
> Bodies enraptured by the abounding earth,
> As whose children we are brethren: one.
>
> And any moment may descend hot death
> To shatter limbs! Pulp, tear, blast
> Beloved soldiers who love rough life and breath
> Not less for dying faithful to the last.
>
> . . . .
>
> Was there love once? I have forgotten her.
> Was there grief once? Grief yet is mine.
> O loved, living, dying, heroic soldier,
> All, all, my joy, my grief, my love, are thine! [2]

[1] *Farewell to Place of Comfort*, Robert Nichols.
[2] *Fulfilment*, Robert Nichols.

The poet's mood is no longer heroic. He has turned away from the bravura and the exaltation of the early days—or has he passed beyond them?—the emotion that inspired *Blow out, you bugles* . . . and *Happy now I go.* He has seen the face of War: and the sight has driven him to a theme which may be lowlier but is surely nearer to the ultimate springs of his own human nature. It is a two-part theme, simple but susceptible of endless variation: " This is my brother—look on his dead face." And if anyone is disposed to deprecate the change of emphasis in the belief that the more exalted theme must necessarily produce the greater poetry, long ago Mrs. Barrett Browning answered that, in one of the rare moments when she rose superior to the vapours of mid-Victorian sentiment. If we drag our memories, her lines may be familiar. She was writing of the great Athenian dramatist, of whom in his own day the traditionalists said exactly the same thing.

> Our Euripides, the human—
> With his droppings of warm tears;
> And his touches of things common
> Till they rose to touch the spheres . . .[1]

That is wise criticism: and it does not apply to ancient Greece alone.

The best and in the truest sense the most exalted poetry of the War came after the mud of Flanders and Loos and Arras and the Somme had brought the poets down to earth. Limed in that thick stinking glue they had time to discover in themselves beneath the soldier the essential human being. The fury of patriotism, the healthy hate of the designated enemy, still

[1] *Wine of Cyprus*, Elizabeth Barrett Browning.

raged at home, but very little of it crossed the Channel. 1914 was over, the high adventure had faded. It was to the individual that men's thoughts turned now, the "loved, living, dying, heroic soldier", the unimaginable horrors and (on off-days when horror took a holiday) the deadly monotony of discomfort which he endured from day to day. In consequence all that later poetry, (all of it that is real and not sham), is dominated by the human but most unsoldierly emotions of tenderness and pity:

> For by my glee might many men have laughed,
> And of my weeping something had been left,
> Which must die now, I mean the truth untold,
> The pity of War, the pity war distilled . . .[1]

or else by a savage bitterness which is the obvious reflex of pity:

> Remembering how he saw those Germans run,
> Screaming for mercy among the stumps of trees:
> Green-faced, they dodged and darted: there was one
> Livid with terror, clutching at his knees . . .
> Our chaps were sticking 'em like pigs . . . " O hell!"
> He thought—" there's things in war one dare not tell
> Poor father sitting safe at home, who reads
> Of dying heroes and their deathless deeds." [2]

If you compare this with Robert Nichols' *Fulfilment*, you notice at once a difference both in texture and atmosphere, or, in plainer words, in the " feel " of the two poems and the general impression which you get from them. It is not that the angle of vision is different (as it definitely is in *Farewell to Place of Comfort*). Spiritually Nichols has passed beyond 1914. Ex-

[1] *Strange Meeting*, Wilfrid Owen.
[2] *Remorse*, Siegfried Sassoon, *Selected Poems*.

perience, that greatest of all teachers with the exorbitant fees, has brought him down to earth. His thoughts are centred upon the common man, the burden-bearer. "This is my brother . . .". But when it comes to putting them into words, he takes us back into 1914 again. The wine is new but the bottle comes from the traditional cellar. The play is over, Mr. Gass has come down from the stage: but he is still in his make-up and still dressed in the costume in which he so convincingly played the Pirate King. . . .

Turn now to Sassoon. With him we part company finally with *Poems of To-day*. True, there is included in the war section with which the "Second Series" opens one poem of his, the much-anthologized and much-belauded *Everyone Sang*.

> Everyone suddenly burst out singing;
> And I was filled with such delight
> As prisoned birds must find in freedom
> Winging wildly across the white
> Orchards and dark green fields; on; on; and out of sight.
>
> Everyone's voice was suddenly lifted,
> And beauty came like the setting sun.
> My heart was shaken with tears, and horror
> Drifted away . . . O, but everyone
> Was a bird; and the song was wordless; the singing
> will never be done.

For all its popularity and (we may grant) its genuine merit this is not his high-water mark—or indeed anywhere near it. A drift of sentiment exhales from it, as from the pot-pourri bowl of Mr. Beverley Nichols' grandmother. It will never, I imagine, lose its place in future anthologies: but it will stand in the same relation to the best of his work as does *Innisfree* to the mature and later Yeats.

But when you come to *Remorse* (which is not included in *Poems of To-day*), you enter a different atmosphere. There is no longer any suspicion of sweet fragrance breathing from the past. There is no looking back to 1914 and the glamour of the old "poetical" tradition. The poet's theme is war in relation to the common man—or the common man in relation to war, whichever way you like to put it: and his whole endeavour is to express his thought as plainly and clearly and as trenchantly as he can; which means, in simple and direct language as near as is humanly possible to the ordinary speech of the common man. He turns his back upon the past, exactly as once a century and more earlier Wordsworth turned his, when with *Lyrical Ballads* he issued a challenge to eighteenth-century tradition. We have already in our first chapter quoted from the preface to that volume, but it is so peculiarly applicable in the present connexion that it will bear quoting yet again.

"The principal object was to choose incidents and situations from common life and to relate them, throughout, as far as possible in a selection of language really used by men . . . My purpose was to imitate and, as far as possible, adopt the very language of men . . . I have wished to keep the Reader in the company of flesh and blood. . . ."

You need not a word changed. It so exactly represents the changed attitude of the poets in the later stages of the War. There was no glamour about existence in a mud-hole, and precious little exaltation: but there was flesh and blood, in plenty. No wonder, then, that they turned to a plain uncompromising realism in expression, to match the crude reality which was life as they were seeing and living it daily. Since their thoughts were all concentrated upon the common man, how could they be expected to view the War from any other angle? They saw it with a passionate singleness of vision—in the words of the Litany, battle, murder, and sudden death. And from this it was but one step to add the response which naturally follows —"From battle, murder, and sudden death, good Lord deliver us".

Hence arises the paradox that the best poetry of the War is the most fiercely anti-war.

This violent emotional reaction affected the poets in different ways. It turned, for instance, Sassoon to satire. If you study his early poetry—pre-war and as far into the War as 1916—you find it quiet and gentle, rather like a typical English landscape by Constable, obviously the work of a highly sensitive mind. Some of it perhaps a little reminiscent: slightly of Blunden, as in *Before Day*, and undisguisedly of Housman in the very Shropshire-laddish *Morning Glory*. But abruptly there comes a change—a full sea-change into something rich and strange, which at a stroke transforms him into one of the great poets of the War. It is sudden and complete, like blowing a smouldering coal into a blaze or (to use a more modern analogy) like the ignition of a petrol dump.

> I walk the secret way
> With anger in my brain.
> O music through my clay,
> When will you sound again? [1]

[1] *A Mystic as Soldier: Selected Poems*. Siegfried Sassoon.

What is this "anger in the brain" but the fierce reaction of a sensitive and imaginative spirit looking at war through the spectacles of pity and hating what it sees? Granted it is a one-sided outlook—but not more so (less perhaps it may seem to us to-day), than the outlook of the early days. Set the two side by side. Consider Rupert Brooke and the suspicion of Ajax-defying-the-lightning which haunts the five sonnets, or Hardy's

> Press we to the field ungrieving . . .[1]

Then take Sassoon:

> You smug-faced crowds with kindling eye
> Who cheer when soldier lads march by,
> Sneak home and pray you'll never know
> The hell where youth and laughter go.[2].

There is no "Emotion recollected in Tranquillity" about either the one or the other: (that is impossible in anything written actually during a war). But these later war-poems of Sassoon have a savage and bitter intensity, a naked scorching sincerity, which cannot be matched in English literature until one goes back to Swift. "Ubi saeva indignatio . . .". You remember how that celebrated epitaph runs. We might fairly translate without doing violence to the Latin: "Here rests the body of Jonathan Swift, where the 'anger in my brain' no more has power to tear my heart to pieces."

But "music through my clay"—if this means anything, it must mean the old "poetical" diction and rhythm, the familiar fragrance of faded leaves.

[1] *Men who march away: Song of the Soldiers.* Thomas Hardy.
[2] *Suicide in Trenches: Selected Poems.* Siegfried Sassoon.

It seems odd to us now, with our knowledge after the event, to find a man standing on the brink of such tremendous and forceful poetry, yet casting one longing lingering look behind. But in 1916, with the old tradition enjoying a new lease of life and the new movement of pre-War days almost universally despised and rejected, it was natural for a poet to be a little doubtful about making a fresh breakaway, and modelling himself not on the glamorous past but on the ordinary up-to-date common natural speech of men.

And Wilfrid Owen, the other indisputably great poet produced by the War, who like Sassoon was blown into genuine flame by pity and horror, had the same doubts about himself.

"Above all," he wrote in the skeleton of a Preface which he left unfinished at his death, "above all I am not concerned with Poetry.

> My subject is War, and the pity of War.
> The Poetry is in the pity. . . ."

This—and indeed the whole of the rest of it—is no more than a series of jottings, fragments of thoughts which he would have expanded, had he lived, into something more coherent and less contradictory; but what he was thinking is clear enough. "This book," the Preface begins, "is not about heroes . . . Nor is it about deeds, or lands, nor anything about glory, honour, might, majesty, dominion, or power, except War." In other words, he can no more write about any of the things which according to the old tradition were considered fit material for poetry. He has broken with that tradition. "Above all I am not concerned with 'Poetry'." What does concern him is to make other people see what he is seeing in the way in which he sees it. And that way is neither pleasant nor glamorous nor exalted.

> If in some smothering dreams, you too could pace
> Behind the wagon that we flung him in,
> And watch the white eyes writhing in his face,
> His hanging face, like a devil's sick of sin;
> If you could hear, at every jolt, the blood
> Come gargling from the froth-corrupted lungs
> Bitter as the cud
> Of vile, incurable sores on innocent tongues,—
> My friend, you would not tell with such high zest
> To children ardent for some desperate glory,
> The old Lie: Dulce et decorum est
> Pro Patria mori.[1]

This (not only in thought, but in expression) is a long way from the poetry of the beginning of the War. (Compare it with Rupert Brooke's rich brocade.) On the other hand, it is very near to the natural speech of men. That vigorous and realistic language sets no distance between the reader and what the poet is intending to convey: and the result is the same impression of intense and naked sincerity which you get from the best of Sassoon.

Owen, of course, was much more than a simple realist. He had a power of arresting phrase that was more than the mere ability to hit on a neat conjunction of words or find a cruder and more startling synonym for a humble spade. For example, in *Mental Cases* his shell-shocked patients wake at morning and (unforgettably, once you have read the line):

> Dawn breaks open like a wound that bleeds afresh.

[1] *Dulce et Decorum est: Poems.* Wilfred Owen.

His diction is his own, and individual. It is not subservient to tradition of lexicon or grammar. In this respect he reminds us of Gerard Hopkins. He uses words with the same imaginative freedom, the same indifference to academic convention. Take this, for instance, again from *Mental Cases*:

> Always they must see these things and hear them,
> Batter of guns and shatter of flying muscles,
> Carnage incomparable, and human squander,
> Rucked too thick for these men's extrication.

He was further a scholar and a craftsman of very great subtlety, with a feeling for rhythm which remains infinitely delicate even when he is at his most savage and brutal. "He was," says Mr. Blunden, in the admirable and sympathetic Memoir which he has prefixed to his edition of Owen,[1] "an unwearied worker in the laboratory of word, rhythm, and music of language, partly by nature and partly from his close acquaintance with French poetry and its exacting technical subtleties . . ."

"One cannot be sure," says Mr. Blunden further, "when he thought out the use of assonances, instead of rhymes, which he perfected. What he made of it is felt at its fullest, perhaps, in the solemn music of *Strange Meeting*, but again and again by means of it he creates remoteness, darkness, emptiness, shock, echo, the last word."

Listen for a moment to a strain of that solemn music. (*Strange Meeting* stands last in the collected volume. Possibly it was his actual swan-song. At any rate, he was working on it up to the time of his death.)

[1] *The Poems of Wilfrid Owen*, edited with Memoir and Notes by Edmund Blunden.

Mark the ebb and flow of the rhythm: like Virgil's epigram on the character of woman, "varium et mutabile semper". Superficially it is the old conventional iambic—(count five feet of a short and a long syllable each)—but it is so counterpointed, as Hopkins would have said, as almost to become a rhythm of pure stress. With the old poetry one consistent rhythm pervades the whole poem, a framework into which the writer fits his thought: but here the rhythm follows the thought, prepared, so to speak, to start afresh with every change of mood, as fluid and adaptable as the mind of an experienced politician. And mark too the curious effect of the assonance rhyme which by never satisfying yet completely satisfies the ear:

> Now men will go content with what we spoiled.
> Or discontent, boil bloody, and be spilled,
> They will be swift with swiftness of the tigress,
> None will break ranks, though nations trek from progress.
> Courage was mine, and I had mystery,
> Wisdom was mine, and I had mastery;
> To miss the march of this retreating world
> Into vain citadels that are not walled.

Owen was killed in action on 4th November, 1918. One week later came the Armistice, and the War was over. These lines of his make a fitting introduction to the period that followed.

CHAPTER V

The Years of Disillusion. T. S. Eliot

THERE was once a *bon mot*, coined in a light-hearted moment, to the effect that no sooner had the War ended than Peace broke out; but it soon ceased to be a jest, even a stale one, as men began to realize how near it came to the plain unpalatable truth.

When will you ever, Peace, wild wooddove, shy wings shut,
Your round me roaming end, and under be my boughs?
When, when, Peace, will you Peace? I'll not play hypocrite
To own my heart. I yield you do come sometimes; but
That piecemeal peace is poor peace. What pure peace allows
Alarms of wars, the daunting wars, the death of it? [1]

This is Gerard Hopkins and it is dated 1879. He was, of course, writing purely of himself, of the conflict in his own soul ("bitter would have me taste . . ."); but he might have been speaking of the years after the War. His lines so exactly express what men were thinking—or beginning to think, when after the first burst of relief and rejoicing they had time to look round and see what kind of an aftermath the War had left behind.

Peace was what everyone most passionately desired: a peace, moreover, that should be both lasting and secure. At first the prospect appeared quite reasonably fair. The struggle was over. The troops had come back with one settled conviction in their minds—a conviction bought with bitter experience at first hand

[1] *Poems*, Gerard Manley Hopkins, 2nd edition, No. 22.

and shared by countless mothers and fathers and wives—that never under any circumstances must such a thing be allowed to happen again. Indeed at the time it seemed almost incredible that it ever should. It did not seem possible that all that suffering and all that sacrifice should in the sequel count for nothing: that Wilfrid Owen's despairing prophecy could actually prove true and men

> go content with what we spoiled

or ever again

> discontent, boil bloody and be spilled.

On the contrary, it seemed that a new world, based on saner and more enlightened counsels, was coming into being. " The War to end War " became a phrase: and more people than one might imagine pinned their faith to it.

But Owen was right and the optimists wrong. You cannot found a peace upon punishment. A man reaps what he sows—like the Theban King, in the old Greek story, who sowed the royal home-farm with dragon's teeth and gathered to his great discomfiture a monstrous crop of bloody-minded men-at-arms.

Even so the Treaty-makers. The mountain went into labour and produced—nothing so innocent as Horace's "ridiculous mouse",[1] but the post-War era of gradual awakening to a disillusion which was all but complete. Mr. A. C. Ward, in his able and comprehensive review of the period which immediately followed the War (*The Nineteen-Twenties*), flatly calls it the " Decade of Despair ", and looking back in the light of what

[1] For the benefit of exact scholars: " Parturiunt montes, nascetur ridiculus mus," Horace, *Ars Poetica, The Art of Poetry*, l. 139.

actually happened, who is going to say that his language is too strong? All the hopes which at the beginning had been so fondly and so confidently cherished, one by one in course of time were broken and proved vain. Instead of the new world chastened into charity by mutual suffering, of which men had dreamed, they found themselves living in a world which day by day revealed a closer and more sinister likeness to the old. Instead of the halcyon period of tranquillity which seemed possible and even probable in the early days of 1919, there followed no real tranquillity at all, but

> Alarms of wars, the daunting wars, the death of it.

All this is a matter of history. There is no need to dot the i's and cross the t's. Some of us can do that for ourselves out of our own private recollections: and anyone who has forgotten or was too young in those days to remember clearly should read Mr. A. C. Ward's admirable summary in his first chapter. We need only notice how the poets were affected by the peculiar circumstances of the time.

Naturally they took colour from the prevailing atmosphere. One of the commonest criticisms of post-War poetry (which you hear both from out-and-out opponents and from would-be friends who "want to like it", if they could, but they really can't!), is that it is neither cheerful nor inspiring. Certainly it is not, but could anyone reasonably expect that it should be either? We have seen the mood of the poets in the latter days of the War, their savage bitterness, their furious and impotent disgust with the hobble in which the whole world seemed caught. In that same mood they entered upon the Peace, determined at all costs to see clearly with eyes unclouded by sentiment or passion.

> Though we are a battered and rather bitter set
> Still we have faced the facts, we have been pretty honest.[1]

How was it possible for any of them during those years of steady and progressive disillusion to write with optimism and yet remain sincere? Even that incorrigible little Ray of Sunshine, Browning's Pippa, would have found it hard work to sustain the burden of her theme-song,

> God's in His heaven,
> All's right with the world.

There was of course the Road to Innisfree: the Way of Escape, of going apart like a little child into the garden and saying "let's pretend!" But the principal aim of the New Movement (have we not seen this clearly?) when it broke with tradition, was to put an end to that kind of unreality: to bring Poetry down from the clouds, or (if you like) to call her in from the garden where she had been playing all too long. "I have wished to keep the Reader in the company of flesh and blood. . . ." Therefore you must expect to find the post-War disillusion reflected in the poetry of the post-War years.

But you find more than disillusion. You find something very nearly approaching chaos. And this too is only what you would naturally expect. The outbreak of war had restored certainty, a belief without question in certain fundamentals—since every nation was fervently proclaiming with one united voice, "I believe

[1] Richard Aldington, *The Eaten Heart*, quoted by Mr. A. C. Ward on title page of *The Nineteen-Twenties*.

in God and Justice and in My Country and the Justice of Our Cause". But when the War went on too long and that certainty gradually disappeared, the inevitable result was a swing in the opposite direction, a return to the general scepticism of pre-War days. The tide came flowing back with all the greater force because of the temporary check which it had received—like the return of the devils to the house which had been swept and garnished. The old world, men hoped and believed, had been swept away with all its mistakes and misconceptions: but with them went also its totems and its gods; its standards and its ideals. Something, of course, had to be put in their place, but since all tradition had gone by the board and precedent was everywhere rejected as outworn and useless either for help or guidance, what test was there left to the new-world builders of soundness or of truth? Only one—the scientific test. Does it work? If so, keep it: if not, cast it aside.

And what effect had this upon poetry? Very much the effect of a triple cocktail upon a life-long abstainer.

It was a break-out rather than a breakaway. Viewed in retrospect it reminds you of one of those regrettable incidents which do occur at times even in the best-regulated of prisons, a group of mutineers established on the roof, gleefully hurling slates at law and order down below and very well aware that every gesture is in full view of a scandalised world outside the walls. The poets were out of hand. "Oh dear, oh dear," the outside world exclaimed, "how crude, how undisciplined, how positively WANTON! New movements never used to be so violent, so completely lawless. Whatever can be the reason?"

There were several reasons. One of them was the War itself. That was the school in which the poets had learnt their philosophy of the New Freedom (or the New Licence, as you like to look at it): and war is the greatest of opportunists. "Army life," says Kipling somewhere,[1] "teaches no man to cross bridges unnecessarily." That is very true—and furthermore, it teaches a man, when he comes to a bridge that simply must be crossed, not to sit down and try to recollect what the textbook said, but to cross it off his own bat in the shortest, simplest and most expeditious manner that occurs to him. In other words, your soldier of experience acts *ad hoc,* caring nothing for what Napoleon may have done at Jena. And the moral? The scientific test, of course. Does it work? If so, keep it: if not, cast it aside.

One other contributing cause we may perhaps notice, The old traditional doctrine (as expounded, for example. by Hamlet to his players [2]), that Art is Imitation (or Representation), began somewhere about the later '90's to give ground to a new and modern theory that Art is not Imitation at all, but Communication. Since that time the new theory enjoyed a kind of triumphal progress and is now all but supreme. It is an intriguing and attractive theory, especially as it contains so much of the actual truth that anyone might be forgiven for believing it to be wholly true. Ask yourself, in what consists the value of a work of Art? The old answer

[1] Actually in *Traffics and Discoveries: The Comprehension of Private Copper.*

[2] "O'erstep not the modesty of nature: for anything so overdone is from the purpose of playing: whose end, both at the first, and now, was, and is, to hold, as 'twere the mirror up to nature: to show virtue her own feature, scorn her own image, and the very age and body of the time, his form and pressure."—*Hamlet, Prince of Denmark,* Act III Scene 2, *ad. init.*

we all know very well. The value of Art lies in the degree of fidelity with which it presents to us human life and human nature. We look in the artist's mirror and expect to find there something corresponding to our own experience, or at any rate recognizably related to it. " But no!" reply the modernists. " That is completely out of date! What scope does it leave for the originality that is always the mark of genius? Is not the artist gifted with a peculiar, personal and inspired vision which enables him to see both further and more clearly than the ordinary mortal? Art is the Communication of that vision. Its value lies in the artist's power to make other people see things in the way in which he sees them."

This of course is undeniably true. No one doubts that the artist has a peculiar kind of vision, personal to himself, and somehow different from that of Tom, Dick and Harry. Whether this is the whole truth about the nature and value of Art, is another matter; but it is at any rate a theory infinitely flattering to the young and aspiring author. And nothing but good came of it, so long as the poets recognized some kind of relation between themselves and the great writers of the past, which means the recognition that you do not bring to the criticism of a twentieth-century modern an entirely different set of standards from those you would apply, for instance, to an Elizabethan of Shakespeare's day. Even New Movements that break away admit the existence of certain enduring standards by breaking back to " a purer, simpler and more natural utterance ". " Modern Poetry ", the New Movement of 1909–1914, deliberately and confessedly broke back to Donne and Dryden.

But the War destroyed all standards and shattered all belief in continuity. What inevitably followed? If Art were Communication, the only thing that mattered was what the poet wanted to say: and if he both said what he wanted and said it in the way in which he wanted, then that must be the full, perfect and proper expression of his Art. For what standard of reference was there left to him? Only one, as we have seen—the scientific test: Does it work? If so, keep it: if not, cast it aside. And who was to judge whether it did work or not? Only himself, "the onlie begetter . . .".

The consequence is that a great deal of the poetry written after the War is the wildest medley. Glance through the pages of any comprehensive anthology of the period and it impresses you as a kind of Saturnalia.[1] The poets, freed from any responsibility towards the past and accepting only themselves as judges and as judged, rushed headlong into an orgy of experiment. They juggled with new words and new forms: they tried new rhythms in all kinds of combination both possible and impossible, and sometimes no apparent rhythm at all. Some abandoned punctuation altogether (thereby throwing an extra and quite unjustifiable burden upon the unfortunate reader): some punctuated upon anarchist principles all their own: some even went so far as to play tricks with the inoffensive print itself.

There is no need to pursue these extravagances into any greater detail. In themselves they are often exciting and, it must be acknowledged, always enter-

[1] The ancient Roman "Christmas", when all the accepted rules of sober law and order were relaxed: and, as the Latin poet said:

> "For seven days we may behave at our own sweet will
> And after, *arrière pensée* is there none."

taining: but too prolonged a sojourn in that Looking-glass jungle is apt to result in an inability to see the wood for the trees. What we are concerned with is the progress and development of the "New" poetry, the attempt to adjust language and expression to the novelties and complexities of this twentieth century.

But whilst the play-boys of the post-War indulged in an orgy of play, carefree and irresponsible as Shelley's Peter Pan of a skylark, there were not wanting more responsible voices to insist upon the inevitable connexion between the poetry of the moment and the poetry of the past. Though English poetry may have developed in a series of breaks-away mainly in tangential directions, nevertheless the whole remains a continuity. Chaucer is as much a "member of one body" as Tennyson, or (to take a recent star in the modern heaven), Wystan Auden. The broad general lines on which you judge the one will be the same broad general lines on which you judge the other, making allowance, of course, for environment, changed conditions, "Time-surrounds", or whatever name you like to give to the ceaseless progression of the marching mind of man.

Of these voices the most important and the most influential was that of T. S. Eliot. "No poet, no artist of any art," he insisted, "has his complete meaning alone. His significance, his appreciation is the appreciation of his relation to the dead poets and artists. You cannot value him alone. . . . He must inevitably be judged by the standards of the past, not judged to be as good as, or worse or better than, the dead; and certainly not judged by the canons of dead critics. It is a judgment, a comparison, in which two things are measured by each other. To conform merely would be for the new work not really to conform at all; it would not be new, and would therefore not be a work of art." [1]

What could be more salutary and more needed at the time as a corrective to the general belief that the standards of the past were dead and buried, and that all that matters is what the poet wants to say? It was said too with a wisdom and air of authority that reminds us irresistibly of that wise and authoritative Victorian, Matthew Arnold. (Indeed, I think, critically Eliot was to the post-War generation what Arnold was to the latter nineteenth century.)

But Eliot, though he may be one of the most distinguished of modern critics, is primarily a poet. And here we may notice a very curious paradox. "My general point of view," he declares with emphasis in the Preface to *For Lancelot Andrewes*, "may be described as Classicist in literature, Royalist in politics, and Anglo-Catholic in religion." The perfect picture, you would say, of a middle-aged survival from the days of Queen Victoria! And when you read the Critical Essays, the sobriety of them, the general atmosphere of Roman (or Victorian) gravitas, the absence of (to say the least) any noticeable sense of humour seem to confirm the portrait.

But turn to Eliot's poetry. The rather prim schoolmaster, in the direct tradition of that prince of pedagogues, Matthew's father, miraculously disappears, and in his place you find a genuine poet who is also a daring and original pioneer. We have already noticed *The Love-song of J. Alfred Prufrock*, the first really

[1] *Individual Talent: Selected Essays.* T. S. Eliot.

considerable poem of the New Movement in its pre-War days. It was quite new both in form and manner: and it was successful. That is, it succeeded in presenting (or perhaps one should say, partly presenting and partly suggesting) the working of a single mind during a minor crisis of a very ordinary person's life. The incident itself is of no particular importance. Therefore you are left to supply the details for yourself. The whole interest lies in the complication and variety of thoughts and emotions which are at work, like water boiling in a kettle, in the mind of one individual.

The Waste Land, which made its appearance after the War, in 1922, is similar in method. It employs the same characteristically modern technique, the mixture of the old direct presentation and the new indirect suggestion taken over from the Symbolists. But that technique has been improved and enlarged: and the poem itself (not merely in sheer bulk) is on a much bigger scale. Where *Prufrock* deals with a single individual, *The Waste Land* deals with the whole post-War generation. It is an epitome of the " Decade of Despair ", and aims at nothing less than presenting to you all the various cross-currents, emotional, intellectual and psychological, which together contribute to the general atmosphere of that unhappy period. He might have written a history, or a three-volume novel: being a poet, he crowds it all into the narrow compass of 430 odd lines.

The Waste Land is a curiously uneven poem. It tempts one to make the old old joke about the curate's egg. (Having made it, we may pass quickly on.) The power and the beauty of certain parts are beyond question. You may find it a strange new kind of beauty which is not instantly obvious to anyone still thinking in terms of Georgian "prettiness". You may even be prepared to go no further than the Caliph's grudging comment in Flecker's play. "It hath," you may remember he remarks of Hassan's impudent behaviour, "a monstrous beauty—like the hind-quarters of an elephant." But still, you would say "beauty".

Consider, for instance, this:

> What are the roots that clutch, what branches grow
> Out of this stony rubbish? Son of man,
> You cannot say, or guess, for you know only
> A heap of broken images, where the sun beats,
> And the dead tree gives no shelter, the cricket no relief,
>
> And the dry stone no sound of water. Only
> There is shadow under this red rock,
> (Come in under the shadow of this red rock),
> And I will show you something different from either
> Your shadow at morning striding behind you
> Or your shadow at evening rising to meet you;
> I will show you fear in a handful of dust.[1]

Or consider that innocent-seeming little elegy upon the fate of those that go down to the sea in ships whom the sea has claimed for its own. It is the shortest of the separate sections into which the poem is divided. It bears a generic title, "Death by Water", so that you may make no mistake, since on the surface it appears nothing more than a simple "Memorial" to one particular sailor unfortunately drowned at sea.

Death by Water

> Phlebas the Phœnician, a fortnight dead,
> Forgot the cry of the gulls, and the deep sea swell
> And the profit and loss.

[1] *The Waste Land.* T. S. Eliot, § 1, *The Burial of the Dead.*

A current under the sea
Picked his bones in whispers. As he rose and fell
He passed the stages of his age and youth
Entering the whirlpool.
Gentile or Jew
O you who turn the wheel and look to windward,
Consider Phlebas, who was once handsome and tall as you.

This might be an epigram from the Greek Anthology, that ancient treasure-house of masterpieces in cameo. It has the same cool deliberate reticence, the same deceptive chiselled simplicity. And if you ask what has Phlebas, a Phœnician, to do with the post-War world of 1922, the answer is that the "Phœnician sailor" is one of the cards in the Tarot pack: and earlier in the poem we have met

Madame Sosostris, famous clairvoyante.[1]

She was sitting, turning the cards—

Here, said she,
Is your card, the drowned Phœnician sailor,
(Those are pearls that were his eyes. Look!) . . .[2]

[1] *The Waste Land*, § 1, ll. 43 *et seq.*

[2] You will notice that Eliot deliberately draws your attention to Ariel's song in *The Tempest*. He wastes no space by an elaborate reference or even a simile,

"As once
The Bard of Avon made his Ariel sing", &c.

He quotes one line, knowing that thereby he will evoke in your mind all your memories of the whole of that magical little song, and of *The Tempest*, and probably of much more too. You may not think that this method of quotation wholesale and without acknowledgment is legitimate: but you must admit that it is economical—and effective. The difficulty is that it keeps the reader's mind continually at stretch, in case he may take something as original, which is really an un-signposted quotation from another writer. And of course if he does not happen to be familiar with the other writer he may miss the reference altogether. *The Waste Land* is literally stuffed with such unacknowledged quotations and reminiscences: and (for our comfort) we may notice that it is a method which Eliot has subsequently almost entirely abandoned.

When you come across him again in "Death by Water", you are meant to add all the associations of the earlier passage to those roused in you by the later. Unknown, unimportant Phlebas is symbol for all the countless unfortunate who have lost their game of hazard with the sea.

I think no one would question the beauty of this Requiem. On the other hand, there are parts of *The Waste Land* so frankly questionable as to defeat even the Curate's powers of assimilation.

Take, for example, the conclusion of Section I. "The Burial of the Dead":

> There I saw one I knew, and stopped him, crying: Stetson!
> You who were with me in the ships at Mylæ . . .

There is no need to quote further. The remaining six lines contain—an inexplicable corpse apparently planted a year ago by Stetson in his front garden, a very far-fetched reference to Cornelia's distracted outburst in the fifth act of Webster's *White Devil*, and one line lifted whole from the Preface to Baudelaire's *Fleurs du Mal*. Rack your brains, trace the references back to their original: and not one yard nearer are you to comprehension of the author's meaning! This Stetson is the trouble. Who was he? What were the ships? And where was Mylæ? You need not rack your brains. The simple answer is that no one knows or could possibly know, except the author himself and the little circle of friends he may have chosen to let into the secret. Stetson belongs to Mr. Eliot's private world; there he must remain, unless by divine revelation, caviare to the general.[1] This may strike you as the

[1] Or it may be that "Stetson" is a "symbol", used by Mr. Eliot in the manner of the Symbolists to stand for something else unexpressed.

equivalent of keeping a spare ace up one's sleeve. What, you ask, becomes of the theory that Art is Communication?

What indeed?

"The criticism has to be met," says Dr. Leavis in his *New Bearings in English Poetry*, commenting upon *The Waste Land*, "that the poem exists, and can exist, only for an extremely limited public equipped with special knowledge. But that the public for it is limited is one of the symptoms of the state of culture that produced the poem. Works expressing the finest consciousness of the age in which the word 'high-brow' has become current are almost inevitably such as to appeal only to a tiny minority. . . . This amounts to an admission that there must be something limited about the kind of artistic achievement possible in our time: even Shakespeare in such conditions could hardly have been the 'universal' genius!"

I do not in the least believe this. I have too much respect for Dr. Leavis to write him down that horrid thing, an intellectual and æsthetic snob (though after reading his account of the Victorians in *New Bearings* one might well begin to wonder). On the other hand, if you let him lead you by the nose, you find yourself denying to modern poetry anything more than a third- or fourth-rate value. It would not be worth your time or mine. Certainly "Stetson" can only appeal to the tiniest minority: and certainly there are other re-

may be that he has deliberately selected the most unimpressive surname he could think of—"Stetson"—in order that it may stand for "anyone", the most commonplace ordinary member or members of the vast population of London, you, me, or any of our neighbours. But this really comes to the same thing as the invention of a private world, since the "symbol" itself is so obscure as to be to all intents and purposes private.

ferences in *The Waste Land* which are equally sibylline. But " Phlebas " is common coin: and much that seems cryptic at first sight yields to persistence if approached in the right way. After all, there is no necessity that all poetry, in order to be good, should also be easy: only that there should be found in it something for you and me and Everyman, not for a special coterie merely. I find it impossible to believe that any poet, not entirely cretinous, would deliberately choose (all things being equal) to limit the audience to which he wishes to appeal. Art, in this respect, is a kind of Exhibition-mania, as you soon find out if you talk to any of our modern poets, even the most eclectic of them. Nor can I believe that " the state of culture " in this present age is the real villain, and that it inevitably forces the best of its poetry into a narrow and self-conscious isolation. What has happened is rather that the increasing complexity of modern life has compelled the poets to discover a new technique, capable of dealing adequately with it—the old not being adaptable enough. Naturally, being entirely novel and still in the stage of exploration, sometimes this new technique " comes off " (so to speak), and sometimes it does not. When it fails, when only the poet himself or a narrow circle of intimate friends and perhaps a few outsiders with peculiarly agile brains are able to understand what he is trying to say, then he becomes " obscure ": then " the poem exists, and can exist, only for an extremely limited public with special knowledge ". But wherein, dear Brutus, lies the fault? Surely not in force of circumstances or any " state of culture " which necessitates the poet's withdrawal into his own private cloud—but in the poet himself. He has bungled the new technique and made a smudge instead of an intelligible mark.[1]

You may think *The Waste Land* a great poem that will stand the test of time, or—you may not. Either way you will be in good company. But whatever its intrinsic merit, I think there is little doubt that in twenty years' time it will be found to have "dated", as definitely as, say, the earlier plays of Bernard Shaw: that is, both the thought itself and the manner of its expression will be seen to belong wholly to one particular period (in this case the nineteen-twenties), and never to range beyond. It may be that it is recognizably dated already—and this one may say without disparagement. For to deny to a poem the timeless quality of the absolutely first class is by no means to deny it any genius or lasting quality at all. There is one glory of the sun, and another of the moon. . . .

There are, however, other reasons why *The Waste Land* must be considered one of the most important, if not the most important, of all the poems which have been written since the War. No future history of poetry that attempts to cover the New Movement will

[1] Day Lewis, in his *Hope for Poetry*, whilst he approves of the poet's having a private world of his own (indeed he holds it to be necessary under modern conditions), nevertheless recognizes that his ultimate aim is the widest public that he is capable of commanding. This is far nearer to the truth than Dr. Leavis's Intelligentsia in compulsory isolation. "The poet is now seeking to find and establish that central calm, a point from which he may begin to work outward again; and in the process he is bound to be obscure, for he is talking to himself and to his friends—to that tiny, temporarily isolated unit with which communication is possible, with whom he can take a certain number of things for granted . . . In this (i.e. modern) poetry there is a perpetual interplay of private and public meaning: the inner circle of communication—the poet's conversation with his own arbitrarily isolated social group—is perpetually widening into and becoming identified with the outer circles of his environment." (*A Hope for Poetry* C. Day Lewis, p. 27.)

be able to avoid at any rate some notice of it. For it is not only a document of the period: it is the document *par excellence*. Its purpose is to give you a picture of the composite mind of a generation—the generation which succeeded to the legacy of the War. (Dr. Leavis [1] calls it " an effort to focus an inclusive consciousness ": which is another way of saying the same thing). It is not intended to be a narrative of events, or in any sense what we mean by a commentary. Rather, it is a study in psychology—by a poet in the form of poetry: a cross-section of what people were thinking and feeling at a time when thought and emotion were peculiarly confused and disturbed.

And does it succeed or does it fail? The answer is not quite so simple as you might perhaps think. The other day I came across a critical article of some years back upon Eliot and his work (in one of the literary weeklies, I think, though I cannot be certain, as my copy has since drowned itself irrecoverably in the sea of papers on my table). At any rate, it was a full-blooded attack, and the writer selected *The Waste Land* as a special target. His chief points, as I remember, were these. You get from the poem as a whole a strong impression of scrappiness and disorder, " without form and void like original chaos ": you move throughout in a depressing atmosphere of gloom and general hopelessness:

> I think we are in rats' alley
> Where the dead men lost their bones . . .

It exhibits a surface cynicism that suggests reaction from thwarted sentiment and common human tender-

[1] *New Bearings in English Poetry*, p. 95.

ness which have been unable to find their natural outlet: there is a shrinking from the old full-blooded climax, an intentional "making great things small" (study the story of the typist and her City lover,[1] and the climax to which it works:

> When lovely woman stoops to folly and
> Paces about her room again, alone,
> She smoothes her hair with automatic hand
> And puts a record on the gramophone.)

And finally, there is the deliberate avoidance of anything like what used to be called Beauty: or if that kind of beauty should ever be approached, the equally deliberate spoiling of it before it can come to its full flower. Nothing, except the cactus, flowers in the Waste Land.

> Yet there the nightingale
> Filled all the desert with inviolable voice
> And still she cried, and still the world pursues,
> "Jug Jug" to dirty ears.[2]

Now all these are valid points which can be substantiated by reference to the text: but before you gather them into a heap to cast into the adverse scale, pause and consider this. If you were to make a list of the salient characteristics of the period which followed the War, would you not begin with those very points which we have just enumerated in criticism of *The Waste Land*? And the poem, let me remind you again, is not an external commentary upon the psychology of the period, but a reflection of it. In which scale will you now place your heap?

[1] *The Waste Land*: § 3, *The Fire Sermon*, ll. 215–256.
[2] *The Waste Land*: § 2, *A Game of Chess*, ll. 100–103.

There is another reason too for the importance of *The Waste Land.* No other poem since the War (or indeed before it since the New Movement began) has had anything like so powerful and far-reaching an effect upon the subsequent development of modern poetry. Our younger poets to-day do not write like Eliot: they would be monstrously indignant if you so much as hinted that they did. But there is not one who has not been profoundly influenced by him (by the Eliot of *The Waste Land* that is, not the Eliot of the later Anglo-Catholic *Ash-Wednesday* and *The Rock*). The reason is not far to seek. The new technique was designed to deal with intricacies in modern life too unsubstantial or too complicated or too frankly novel to be comprehended by the older direct method. In *Prufrock* it had been employed merely to illumine an individual character at one moment of time; in Pound's *Hugh Selwyn Mauberley* to reveal a personality (a peacock opening for you his oddly decorative tail); but in *The Waste Land* the scale was infinitely enlarged. One saw now the new method under magnification, so to speak, what it was capable of doing and also what it was not. And therefore, even though you may not be wholly convinced by *The Waste Land* as poetry, you cannot afford to neglect it as a landmark in poetry's progress.

But, you say, this new method, this new technique, of which we have been talking so much, should we not be the better for a definition? What is it exactly? How, exactly, did it arise?

That is a fair question. Let us devote a chapter to its nature and origin.

CHAPTER VI

Psychology and Poetry

THE true pioneer of the new poetry of to-day, as we have already noticed, was Gerard Manley Hopkins. Actually he anticipated every major innovation in language, technique and rhythm, which may be claimed as an original discovery in modern practice, with one notable and very important exception. He knew nothing of the revolution effected by modern psychology. This, however, was hardly his fault. For Psychology only came into being as a separate science in the early part of the last century, and it is only within the last thirty years or so that the results of the new study became at all generally known. When they did spread beyond purely specialist circles, they upset a number of venerable apple-carts.

Psychology of course means the science of the mind, and modern psychology ultimately derives from Descartes in the seventeenth century. He first directed attention to the need for an inquiry into the nature and capacity of mind, the instrument upon which all intellectual activities must in the last resort depend. The ancient world—and the thinkers of mediæval times—had fully understood the Fallibility of the Senses. But how if the mind itself were equally fallible—either of its own nature and constitution, or because being resident in the body it might be affected by the disabilities of the body? After Descartes every philosopher found himself obliged at the outset to face this very awkward question. In fact Mind, which had hitherto taken a comparatively back seat, now moved up into the front row. The more you think about this problem, the more there is in it to think about: and by the beginning of the nineteenth century it became clear that a field of inquiry had been opened up which would prove a whole-time occupation in itself. And moreover, since the efforts of the philosophers had not been conspicuously successful, it seemed high time that the more practical methods of science were given a trial. So, gradually and without any flourish of trumpets, Psychology broke away from orthodox philosophy and became a separate science on its own.

I am aware that there are objections to describing Psychology as the science of the mind. For example, we have all been taught that it is very wrong to define one thing in terms of another which is itself insufficiently known. Disputation has always been one of the commonest forms of sublimation amongst the learned: and the psychologists have certainly not shown themselves any more disposed than the philosophers to agree amicably upon a stock definition of what exactly Mind may be. I am aware also that the province of Psychology is by no means limited to an investigation of the mental processes either of human beings or of animals. It extends to the whole question of behaviour and the various ways in which behaviour is conditioned. And " Social Psychology " surveys an even wider field.

But this book, thank goodness, is not a Manual of Psychology. We are solely concerned with the effect which that science has had upon poetry, and indeed upon literature generally, in the present age. We need not follow the agile specialist throughout the tortuous windings of his burrow: it is enough to mark him at the entrance, and at one entrance only. For it is the new information as to the constitution of our individual minds that has so profoundly affected modern writers and artists of every kind. We may therefore confine ourselves to that branch, or those branches of the science which are called "Analytical" and deal specifically with minds and how they work.

And what, after all this preamble, was this new information?

It is not easy to pot an elephant, like Bovril, into a small bottle and at the same time to avoid using language of a fearsome technicality; but in essentials what was new was this. Hitherto Mind had been regarded as an entity, a "something" which willed and felt and thought: existent for all practical purposes upon one plane—that is, the plane of consciousness. Philosophers, of course, had long recognized that there must be a part of Mind, perhaps a very considerable part, which lay below that level. No one could go very far into the problem of knowledge and particularly into the difficulties involved in the fact of memory without being forced into some such supposition. But it remained a supposition, since no one believed that anything could ever be known in the proper sense of the word about what might be below the conscious level. For only what was in the conscious mind could be observed and studied.

The psychologists tried a different method and proceeded to investigate along strictly scientific lines. The results were, as the guide-book says of the inhabitants of the Zoo, "many and various". How various you may see from the number of pages devoted to "Psychology" in any encyclopædia. For instance, there were discovered connexions between mind and body far more intimate than had ever been suspected: and much of the mind's activity, which had previously been assumed without question to be "independent", now appeared to be due to forces over which the mind had no control. But the important step forward (for our purpose) came from the study of the remarkable effects observed in hypnosis, as applied experimentally to the cure of certain nervous disorders, in particular, the alternation of two or even more entirely distinct personalities in one individual mind. Out of this developed the celebrated Freudian Method of psychotherapy, better known perhaps as a recognized branch of psychological investigation under the name of Psycho-analysis. For though Dr. Freud was primarily concerned with the treatment and observation of "mental cases", it was his discovery [1] (unpleasant as it may sound) that the abnormal, even in the most extreme types of neurosis, differs only in degree from the normal, that is from you (I hope) and me.

The result of inquiry along these lines has been a revolution in our outlook. No longer can we believe in that compact little entity with its conveniently indeterminate undertow that could never be studied or known. It is to that undertow that the psychologists have given their special attention. We must think now of Mind as an affair, so to speak, of layers. The topmost, of course, is the old layer of consciousness still with its triple function of thinking and feeling and willing, but of considerably less importance according to modern ideas than it used to be thought in the past.

[1] Vide *The Psychopathology of Everyday Life*, Sigmund Freud.

Below it lies the whole extent of the sub-conscious—or the Unconscious. You may call it which you please: for this is one of the many points upon which the psychologists have not yet made up their minds to agree among themselves. But perhaps (purely for convenience and fully recognizing the inadequacy and even the inaccuracy of our metaphor), we may make two layers of it. There is the sub-conscious, let us say, immediately below the surface: and deeper down, beneath all, the completely unconscious—lying, exactly as the serpent, "Source of All Strength", according to the Indian Vedantas, lies coiled in the lowest part of the human body.[1]

But, you say, all this was known before. It is only looking at a familiar object from an unfamiliar angle. What fresh discovery, of interest to the artists, have the psychologists made?

They have made many, some of them mutually contradictory; but that is only to be expected of a new science exploring new ground. We may select two, which are amongst the most important; for whatever modifications in the future may result from further knowledge or fresh evidence, they have had already an incalculable effect upon the form and method of modern poetry.

First, we now know that vague and indeterminate though the sub-conscious still remains, there exists between it and the conscious a constant two-way traffic, like Francis Thompson's

> Traffic of Jacob's ladder
> Pitched betwixt Heaven and Charing Cross.

[1] Need I point out that this is not fairy story but metaphor?

And out of this arises the second. We know something (not very much, but something) of the contents of the sub-conscious mind. There are thoughts and feelings which appear to belong to the constitution of the mind itself: and there are thoughts and feelings which have been put down there out of the conscious, as one puts away in the attic unwanted luggage or on occasion anything not considered quite suitable for visitors to see. All or any of these may share in the traffic: may float up to the surface, either unbidden, like " drowned faces in a pool ", or they may be deliberately evoked. We all know " how one thing suggests another ". That is the technique of evocation. Up they come, each linked with another down below: and that in its turn hooks another, and so on and so on. One thing further may be observed: there need not necessarily be any community or even any connexion between the separate units in the procession, excepting only the actual link itself; and that may be and often is so slight that to the rational mind it would seem hardly capable of forming any link at all. This whole process (in gross and obviously inadequate physical metaphor), is what is known as " Free Association ".

If you open a window, you expect a change of atmosphere (and incidentally you expect an outburst of temper from any old gentleman whose warm and fuggy comfort has been suddenly disturbed). So with all this new information, which was in effect like a window opening up for poetry a new and most exciting stretch of country.

" Free Association " in itself, of course, is only the process by which Suggestion works: and Suggestion, as we have already noticed when speaking of the

Symbolists, has always been one of the recognized methods by which poetry obtains its effects. What was new was the rationalization of the process. You may compare it to what happens after a war, when the army authorities after due meditation issue a drill-book based upon manœuvres which were carried out by the light of nature whilst the war was on. You find, therefore, in modern poetry a much more deliberate attempt to explore the world-below-the-surface, based upon the drill-book provided by Psychology: and you find methods of evocation which are bound to seem strange and *outré* because they go beyond anything that was known before.

Take the old method. Take Macbeth on the eve of Duncan's murder standing at the window and watching the night draw on:

> Light thickens; and the crow
> Makes wing to the rooky wood . . .[1]

[1] *Macbeth*, Act III, Scene 2—Who cares that, strictly speaking, a Crow is not a Rook? How many even know the difference? Shakespeare himself, knowing that he was going to use " rooky " in the next line, chose a synonym —or at any rate a word very often loosely used for " rook " in common speech. Is there any more to it? Mr. William Empson, however, in his *Seven Types of Ambiguity* subjects these two lines to a very careful and detailed analysis (pp. 23–25) and goes a great deal further. He concludes thus: " Rooks live in a crowd and are mainly vegetarians; crow may be either another name for a rook or it may mean the Solitary Carrion Crow. This subdued pun is made to imply here that Macbeth, looking out of the window, is trying to see himself as a murderer, and can only see himself as in the position of the crow . . . that he has to distinguish himself from the other rooks by a difference of name, Rook-Crow, like the kingly title; only, that he is anxious, at bottom, to be at one with the other rooks, not to murder them . . ." I cannot go as far as this with Mr. Empson. Shakespeare could be subtle, but this does not seem to me Shakespeare's kind of subtlety. "Personally," says Mr. Empson, " I am pleased and given faith by this analysis, because it has made something which seemed to me magical into something which seems to me sensible." Exactly—but it is possible to carry analysis of poetry so far as to analyse away the poetry altogether.

The whole is haunted with overtones; and the single epithet " rooky " in itself conjures up an almost infinite succession of associative images and thoughts. In their context, of course, the lines are part of a longer speech. We are hurried on, so that we are actually conscious of no more than a proportion of these thoughts and images: but they are all there under the surface, or (as one says) " at the back of the mind ". Pause, and without bothering about the rest of the speech let them drift freely through the mind. What end is there to them, until you yourself choose to apply the closure? They are of all sorts and kinds, from clamorous rookeries in quiet country places even to the utterly delectable flavour of young rook pie.

Set beside this a modern example of evocation:

> Vacant shuttles
> Weave the wind.[1]

There is the same raising of ghosts here. The same kind of phantom procession musters at the gates of the mind. Words are being used to mean more than they appear to mean. The sentence as a whole is greater than itself.

It is the same, but there is a difference.

With the old method you expect to find—and you do find—each sentence capable of bearing a perfectly straightforward surface meaning, however various and subtle may be the further implications intended. Macbeth looks out upon the evening and remarks that the rooks are making their way home, which we all

[1] From *Gerontion*, T. S. Eliot.—I selected this in particular as a modern example, because Dr. Leavis says of it, " only an analysis on Mr. Empson's lines could be anything like fair to the subtleties of the poem ". (*New Bearings in English Poetry*, p. 86.)

know to be their habit when dusk begins to fall; but who ever heard of a vacant shuttle that had a habit of weaving the wind? No one, of course. It was not the modern poet's intention that anyone should. The surface meaning is not important. What matters is the under-meaning, which the specially chosen oddly assorting words evoke.

Perhaps an objection strikes you here. If the poet means not what he says but what he implies, will not the result be many meanings instead of one? For what lies below the surface is not one definite idea, but a whole flock of associated thoughts, not necessarily (as we have seen) homogeneous, and connected only in the very loosest way. This of course is true. It is a difficulty inherent in the method. But taken as a whole, such thoughts and suggestions usually have a definite character, a general identity even in their individual difference. For instance, if one exclaims " Alas!" you would hardly say that the general trend of the thoughts which it suggests to you is either cheerful or comic, although it is perfectly possible that Dan Leno or a music hall or a funny story might occur somewhere in the sequence. There is no strict logical censorship in the Kingdom of the Sub-conscious Mind. Rather, if you read the psychologists, there is a kind of Wonderland irresponsibility, which reminds you of a nursery party when Nurse is out of the room.

But to return to our shuttles—you realize that the poet is intending to suggest; and provided you do not bother too insistently about any literal surface meaning, you realize also the general character of the suggestion which he intends. You let your imagination run free and so you get your meaning.

Gerontion is a sketch of the mind of an old man in reverie. Once he was young. ("In the juvescence of the year came Christ the tiger.") Religion and Desire were at war within him, once. He remembers fragments, bits of the past: incidents, people he has met. A Japanese gentleman: a lady—he remembers a gesture of hers: another lady who gave him a look in the days when he was young. Just that much he can remember. No more. It is too much trouble for a tired old brain. His thoughts flow aimlessly on:

> Vacant shuttles
> Weave the wind.

How much does this, which at first may seem to say nothing, really say to you?

And from the sentence with the under-surface meaning it is only a step to the half-sentence and the single word.

> Whether the man living or the man dying
> Whether this man's dead life, or that man's life dying
> His real life a fading light his real death a light growing.
> Whether the live dead I live with. . . .

This is the beginning of Stephen Spender's *Vienna*. Two half-sentences, you observe with your nose for grammar, uncompleted, like lopped branches of a tree left waving in the air. How can they mean anything, with no principal verb to "make sense" of them? And if you read on, with hope in your heart, you get no further help. The poem proceeds thus:

> Ladies of the Pension
> Beaurepas, their kind gray cropped love prattling
> Amongst diseases. " I think an operation
> At the North Pole where this world is all white flesh

> Is dear, if you love him." And at the head of our table
> Mister proprietor, oh our king and prime minister
> Our wet dream dictator, our people's president
> Printed in papers and cut out with scissors,
> Dead man living, bald bobbing cork . . .

These of course are " the live dead I live with ", in the Pension Beaurepas, in Vienna; and how vivid and actual they are, the ladies and the little bald-headed proprietor! But there remain the first four lines, meant, you observe by the two full-stops, to be complete in themselves:

> Whether the man living or the man dying
> Whether this man's dead life, or that man's life dying . . .

Later we are told that there is a man dying after being operated on in hospital,

> His life sinking, and his real life decaying
> His wound a wound, his life a life, his death
> Opening to life like a flower him overarching . . .

It is Vienna, the Vienna of Dolfüss and Major Fey and Stahremberg. The Workers' Putsch against the Government has failed, and bloodily failed. That is the theme of the whole poem.

A man lies dying of his wounds in hospital, " his wound a wound ":

> Whether the man living or the man dying . . .
> Whether the live dead I live with . . .

These two lines are the leit-motif of the preliminary section of the poem. They are repeated at its close. Certainly it has the effect of ending a piece of music on an unresolved discord; but do you really need the poet to resolve it for you? Cannot your own imagination running free do that as well and better than a plain statement in black and white? I would remind you of that remark of Mallarmé's, which we quoted earlier in the book: "My aim is to evoke an object in deliberate shadow, without ever actually mentioning it. . . ."

And the evocative single word, standing in place of a sentence by itself, is no new thing—as, for instance:

> The Campbells are coming. Hurrah! Hurrah!

The innovation is the use of single words in isolation, which have no apparent relevance to their context at all. Not until you look beneath the surface and let flow into your mind the stream of thoughts and feelings and memories and what-not else from the sub-conscious, do you perceive that they have any connexion with the rest of the poem.

Obviously "Free Association", this deliberate exploitation of what lies below the conscious level, must have had a very considerable influence upon the technique of poetry. It is a method, one must remember, which is still in the experimental stage. The result at present has been similar to what happens when a new and powerful drug is first introduced into clinical practice. Where it succeeds, it succeeds magnificently (as for instance the closing passage, ll. 422–433, of *The Waste Land*, or the first and the final sections of Spender's *Vienna*). But it also has its dangers.

One of them is the often unmanageable and sometimes unpredictable character of the associations aroused, though we need not agree with Mr. Day Lewis in accepting this as inevitable. "The process," he says, referring to Free Association, "makes things difficult for the reader, because his associations with any given idea or image are probably different from those of the poet, and he is likely to feel as puzzled and uncomfortable as if he were listening to some one talking in his sleep."[1] If this held good in all cases and on all occasions, then clearly any modern poet would be a fool to have anything to do with so stultifying a method. He wants to communicate—but Free Association at once puts him at cross-purposes with his reader.

But though this can and does happen, there is no necessity that it should. Often, as a matter of plain fact, it does not. When the new drug works, it works to the satisfaction of all concerned: that is, the poet himself and you and me. It is true that the reader's associations with any given idea or image are seldom identical with those of the poet. Perhaps they never are; but we were agreed (I hope) that there is a kind of general identity in the chain of thoughts and images conjured up by evocative words and phrases. It was this that made "Vacant shuttles weave the wind" intelligible in its context to the reader, as it was to the poet who wrote it, though the actual sequence of ideas evoked in both cases is quite certainly not the same.

This is really only a restatement of the ancient maxim that great poetry has a universal appeal,[2] because the ideas with which it deals and the emotions upon which it plays are fundamental and common to

[1] *A Hope for Poetry*, Cecil Day Lewis, p. 20.

[2] I do not mean of course universal in the sense that great poetry is read in every home in England: only in the sense that it is never the private affair of one small coterie which is alone able to appreciate and understand it. If this is the case, then (*pace* Dr. Leavis and Mr. Day Lewis), there must be something wrong with the poetry.

all mankind. Modern psychological jargon would express this differently; but the substance remains the same. Even though the poet is trying to evoke not one definite idea but a complex of thoughts and memories and emotions, the question for him still is—do they touch the common humanity in man? That is, have they the same general character in the mind of every reader who responds to the evocation? If they have, the reader will not feel as if he were "listening to someone talking in his sleep". If he does feel that (and one must admit that very often he does), then the poet has made one of two mistakes, and possibly both. Either he is trying to suggest a range of associated ideas which is petty, small and peculiar to himself (his own little private world), or he has bungled the key to the evocation, making it a "symbol" which has significance only for himself: or a reference in some language with which the reader happens not to be acquainted (*The Waste Land* quotes with embarrassing freedom from Latin, French, German and Italian, and we cannot all be expected to have the gift of tongues): or it may be a reference in our own language so recondite that no ordinary reader could be expected to have come across it, for instance, Eliot's frequent echoes of the minor Elizabethan dramatists, with whose works anyone could be excused for being unfamiliar.

But this is not the only danger in the application of the new drug to modern practice. Evocation is a method of tapping the vast resources of the subconscious, as one taps a barrel of beer; but unlike beer, the stream from below flows better from a small tap than from a large one. "Turn but a stone and start a wing!"[1] As with the Imagists, so with the Evocators who succeeded and superseded them (as we have seen), the motto is, "Minimum of Means to produce Maximum of Effect". Logically therefore the ideal poem, according to the modern method, should consist of a series of isolated ejaculations, preferably highly evocative vigorous single words, like the back-firings of a recalcitrant motor-bicycle. Which, to misquote Euclid's formula, is absurd.

Of course it is absurd—but consider for a moment the final passage in *The Waste Land*.

> Quando fiam ceu chelidon—O swallow swallow
> Le Prince D'Aquitaine à la tour abolie
> These fragments have I shored against my ruins
> Why then Ile fit you. Hieronymo's mad againe.
> Datta. Dayadhvam. Damyata.
> Shantih shantih shantih.

If you wanted to be nasty, would you describe this so very differently? Is it not "a series of isolated ejaculations"? It is; but it is also the closing passage of the whole poem. Each isolated phrase is intended to evoke something (more than "something", a whole complex of ideas and images), with which if you have read the poem you will be familiar.[2] You could not

[1] If my evocative quotation has failed of its effect and you have missed the reference, you will find it in Francis Thompson's *Kingdom of God*.

[2] With the exception of Datta, Dayadhvam, Damyata (explained for you in Eliot's own notes), none of these evocative phrases and words refers directly back to any particular passage in the poem. They are reminiscences of other poems—and plays. For instance, the first is from the *Pervigilium Veneris*, a late-Latin poem of uncertain authorship and date: the second is a reminiscence of one of the lyrics in Tennyson's *Princess*: and so on. You have to allow each of them to make its own evocative effect upon you, collect all the hares thus started running about in your mind, and apply the whole complex emotional result to the impression produced on you by the reading of the poem.

set them all down in black and white, partly because they are as many as the stars in heaven and partly because some are so vague and elusive as to defy analysis: nevertheless these are not illusory—you are meant to take them into account. Put them all together and you have a summary of the content of the whole poem, like the "moral" of an old-fashioned bed-time story; but as in the poem itself, so in the conclusion it is implied and not expressed. It remains "an object in deliberate shadow . . .".

But this is a special case. Compression is a two-edged weapon. When it is exaggerated into a sustained staccato, it becomes a definite menace. "Minimum of Means for Maximum of Effect" is a good motto, since compression is one of the essential elements in the making of poetry; but it is not the only element, nor is it the only essential. It is a temptation to a poet, excited and thrilled by the possibilities of the new method, to concentrate upon it to the exclusion of all else. Presumably he satisfies himself; but the result for the reader is like eating an orange from which all the juice has been squeezed.

How often do you feel this about a modern poem, which otherwise might entirely captivate you! You read it and you murmur to yourself (in case one of our modern Intellectuals might overhear), "Oh the little more and how much it is!" I do not mean an absence of Victorian richness, "juiciness" one might say, if one had the courage to be so vulgar: nor the meticulous dry precision of the eighteenth century. I mean more than that. You can observe the same tendency in modern conversation. We talk no longer in graceful periods, but in ellipse, a kind of clipped speech; and a great many of its abruptnesses are highly evocative, just as in the new poetry. (How many different meanings and implications could be assigned to the simple exclamation, "Oh yeah"?) You do not have to look far for an example—even from a poet who can at other times command your genuine assent and admiration.

Easter Monday

The corroded charred
Stems of iron town trees short pure jets
Of burning leaf. But the dust already
Quells their nervous flame: blowing from
The whitening spokes
Of wheels that flash away
And roar for Easter. The city is
A desert. Corinthian columns lie
Like chronicles of kings felled on their sides
And the acanthus leaf shoots other crowns
Of grass and moss. Sand and wires and glass
Glitter in empty, endless suns . . . And
In the green meadows, girls, in their first
Summer dresses, play. The hurdy-gurdy noise
Trumpets the valley, while egg-freckled arms
Weave their game. Children gather
Pap-smelling cowslips. Papers
Weightless as lucid clouds, browse on the hills.
The bulls in tweeds
Hold in their golden spectacles
Twin crystal glasses, the velvet and far
Mountains. Look, holiday hands
From trams, 'buses, bicycles, tramps,
Like one hand coarse with labour, grasp
The furred bloom of their peach.[1]

[1] *Easter Monday*, Stephen Spender, Publ. *New Verse*, No. 17, Oct.-Nov. 1935.

This is Stephen Spender. Compare it with *The Express* (quoted at the end of Chapter III). There you have a steady assured movement, like an elaborate gesture perfectly integrated and harmonious from start to finish. The whole poem is like the engine herself, "gliding like a queen" and "always . . . underneath" (you feel it as you read)

> goes the elate metre of its wheels.

But *Easter Monday* does not glide. It jerks. It is not one gesture, fused and harmonized; but a series of separate gestures. It always seems to me, when I read it (even for the second and third time), as if the poet had had an idea for a poem and rushed to the nearest post office and sent it as a telegram. Or, alternatively, you may think that it reads like a reporter's notes on the spot for an article, "Bank Holiday—City Workers in Rural Haunts".

Or—you may be convinced by it. But even so, I think you will miss something in it, which you find abundantly and to your complete satisfaction in *The Express*.

But we have already reached a full chapter's length and are not done yet with the influence of Psychology. Let us, following the modern method with the child who demands more cake at a tea-party, take another.

CHAPTER VII

More Psychology, Character and Sequence

THE psychologists have split up mind, as the physicists have split the atom. The result of their labours reminds us irresistibly of one of those modern multiple Tube-railway junctions—at Piccadilly Circus, say—that burrow deeper and deeper underground. The analogy is almost perfect. There is the surface and there are mysterious depths. At each successive level flows a constant stream of traffic, and between levels moving stairways provide continuous two-way communication. The whole station is a honeycomb; but ask yourself, which is The Station? Which the supreme, the most important part? Is it the booking-office (which under modern conditions is more than three-parts automatic)—and the circulating area, with subways and stairs connecting with the world outside? Is it lower down, the traffic of the Piccadilly Railway and the busy life that goes on at that level? or below that, the Bakerloo? Or is it something more subterranean still, to which the public never penetrates? . . . Or is it all—that hole in the ground which we call Piccadilly Tube Station, entrances, exits, stairways, levels, depths—one and indivisible, a little Kingdom in which there is no first or last?

Psychology at present is only prepared to give the politician's answer, "Wait and See". Meanwhile mind lies in pieces—surely a most intriguing and fascinating spectacle! Dismemberment (which reveals what was hid and tumbles skeletons out of cupboards) always has a fearful fascination. It satisfies our natural curiosity and at the same time gives us something new to play with. Could you expect any writer, with eyes upon the present and the future rather than the past, not to be thrilled and fascinated by this display of novelties? Could you expect him not to pounce upon the pieces and experiment, knowing full well that though they may be pieces only, they are all part of that complete human nature, which is his proper province, as a writer?

In the past the tendency was all the other way.

Look back only to the last century. The great Victorian novelists, when they came to the delineation of a character, were most concerned with fitting all the pieces into one complete and rounded whole. They recognized of course the complexity of the business; if they had not, they would not have been the capable story-tellers that they were. They knew very well that the ordinary man is rather Shakespeare's Hamlet than plain straightforward Mr. Vice or Mr. Goodheart of the Moralities. They were as fully aware as any modern psychologist, that motives may be mixed, that a man often speaks and acts with the most uncompromising decision, whilst inwardly he plays the children's game of see-saw—" this way and that " (to take an expressive phrase from Tennyson, which he himself lifted bodily from Virgil), " this way and that dividing the swift mind ".[1] All this they understood very well; but their chief aim was to tie up all the loose ends and tuck away any inconvenient stragglers out of sight,

[1] For the benefit of exact scholars, Virg. *Aen.* VIII, l. 20.

so as to give to each of their characters a " character ". And by a "character" they understood something clear-cut and definite, an integrated and coherent whole.

But when you turn the century and come to modern times, you find a marked difference. There are of course plenty of writers still, and good ones too, who remain faithful to the old tradition: but there are others whose eyes are upon the present and the future without one glance behind. Their method, naturally, is different. They make no attempt to portray character in the round, since life itself never presents a personality to us in that way. On the contrary, character comes to us in fragments and bits which we have to put together for ourselves. Therefore the novelist of to-day appears to concentrate his interest not upon the whole but upon the component parts—which are, in fact, those fascinating pieces into which the psychologists have split up mind. All those pieces, according to the modern idea, even though they belong to very different levels, must be taken into account in any full and proper estimate of character. A man acts (or thinks he acts) out of his conscious will: but to know him as he is, we must know also something of the cloud of contradictions that hovers in the background, the cross-currents, the continuous pressure of unconscious forces on him.

And the novelist's technique is different too. He does not comment. He gives you no neat little character sketch, no helpful summary. Rather he is like the master at the beginning of a mathematical hour; he writes down the digits of a complicated addition sum, and leaves you in the light of your own intelligence to find your own answer.

Hardy was the last of the great novelists in the old tradition. He was also nearest in outlook and in feeling to our own time. Compare and contrast, as the examination papers say, his firm and solid characters with any that you please from a modern novel. Compare, for example, his "Tess" with the men and women in Huxley's *Eyeless in Gaza*. Tess comes out of the book a complete figure, as if you had cut round her outline with a pair of scissors and lifted her out whole. When you put down the book, she remains almost terrifyingly real. You not only feel that you know her almost as a living acquaintance: but (and this is the point here) you feel that you know what Hardy himself thought about her and also what he intended you to think. But have you any of the same feelings after reading *Eyeless in Gaza*? Do you feel that you know definitely either what Huxley thinks himself, or what he intends you to think? You do not; you only infer. (You and I of course infer rightly: but it is astonishing how many people otherwise quite intelligent cannot put two and two together but must impute a filthy mind to one of the most savage of our modern Puritans!) The "character" of Huxley's characters is given you in scraps—sometimes clear and consistent, sometimes contradictory, sometimes apparently irrelevant (as our own thoughts often seem to be). And these scraps, we should observe, these "bits and pieces" are by no means all of a kind. They range through all the mental layers which psychology has opened up to us: conscious action and thought, the stream of thought and image running below the surface, the deep Unconscious blindly exerting its powerful influence. Out of these you make your own synthesis; which is as far as the modern writer is prepared to go in giving definite shape to individual character.

One rather striking consequence we may also observe which follows upon the use of this method. The "time-sequence" used to be regarded as something almost sacrosanct, to be played with only at a writer's peril; now it has become of little or no importance. For since the "scraps" themselves are so miscellaneous, it cannot matter to the final synthesis in what order they are presented to the reader. The position of the digits in a single number makes all the difference in the world, but the position of the numbers in a column for addition makes no difference at all. *Eyeless in Gaza* makes no steady progress towards a fixed and appointed end. On the contrary, the narrative skips like a young ram (or perhaps one might say better, leaps like a Douglas Fairbanks), back and forth over different episodes and epochs in its hero's career. . . .

Pass now from prose to poetry. You find the same sharp contrast between To-day and Yesterday. The poets, like the novelists, are interested in the scattered pieces rather than the integrated whole. They too will not be definite: they too leave the ultimate synthesis to you.

Eliot's *Gerontion*, as we have noticed before, is a character-sketch—of an old man, as revealed by himself in monologue.

> Here I am, an old man in a dry month . . .

So he starts: and flows gently on. Now Browning frequently used the same method (the continuous monologue)—and for the same purpose, to sketch a character, to reveal a human being. It is interesting to compare Victorian and modern. You remember perhaps *The Bishop orders his Tomb*[1] (or perhaps you do not. Browning is out of fashion just now: more so, curiously enough, than Tennyson, though one would have expected the more rugged and more intellectual master to have been the first to show signs of returning to favour). It is a monologue nearly twice as long as *Gerontion*. The Bishop is on his deathbed: his called-by-courtesy nephews gather round him, and he speaks.

I can understand anyone at first reading saying that Browning's indomitable lecherous old holy sinner emerges as a personality far more vivid and substantial than Eliot's vague old man, "a dull head among windy spaces". Read Browning once and you know exactly all that he means to tell you. The whole picture is there before your eyes. The dying bishop wandering back into the past—the lady whom once he loved,

> She, men would have to be your mother once:

and Gandolf, fellow-priest and hated rival, still unforgiven: who coveted her too but without success, and dying snatched for himself the one thing which they both coveted more than woman,

> the corner South
> He graced his carrion with, God curse the same!

and so to the end:

> Well go. I bless ye . . .
> And leave me in my church, the church for peace,
> That I may watch at leisure if he leers—
> Old Gandolf, at me, from his onion-stone,
> As still he envied me, so fair she was!

Close the book, and out he steps: so vivid, so actual.

[1] *The Bishop orders his Tomb at Saint Praxed's Church.—Men and Women* R. Browning.

You see him; but ask yourself, do you know him? Or is it that you know only his conscious self, his surface level? What of the under-surface stream of thought and image, the powerful evocations of buried memory and desire, that must be flowing steadily "behind the mind", all the while that he is speaking? He says nothing, you will notice, throughout the whole monologue, which does not come from the top, the conscious level; and at the end there is no adding-up to be done, no further inference is needed. Browning has not left, and never intended to leave anything "in deliberate shadow, without ever actually mentioning it. . . ."

But the monologue in *Gerontion* is all at different levels: or rather, to be accurate, it is the vehicle of thoughts that come from different levels. The modern poet, like Browning, intends a picture of a mind: but, unlike Browning, he wants to show the mind working throughout all its parts. If we may return to our rather cumbrous metaphor, he takes the lid off Piccadilly Circus Station and shines his flashlight from top to bottom down the shaft, so that you see the hive in action at every level. He does not bother about tucking away loose ends, because he believes that loose ends are essential parts of mind as it is. Consequently if *Gerontion* appears somewhat vague and scrappy, and less clear and crisp, when set beside *The Bishop orders his Tomb*, it must be recognized that the modern author intends exactly that vagueness.

Gerontion is not homogeneous (in the sense in which the Browning monologue is). Look for a moment at the different levels. There is the opening:

> Here I am, an old man in a dry month,
> Being read to by a boy, waiting for rain. . . .

That is the top, the surface, the level on which ordinary conversations are conducted; and so it proceeds, until suddenly you find your eyes and nose and mouth under water. There is no warning, no stage-direction, "Selah!",[1] either in the text or in the margin:

> I an old man,
> A dull head among windy spaces.
> Signs are taken for wonders. "We would see a sign!"
> The word within a word, unable to speak a word,
> Swaddled with darkness. In the juvescence of the year
> Came Christ the tiger.
>
> In depraved May, dogwood and chestnut, flowering judas,
> To be eaten, to be divided, to be drunk
> Among whispers. . . .

It is clear that the thoughts here (or fragments of thoughts) come from a different level—if only because of the obscurity of their expression, when read for the first time. Taken literally, they have little or no meaning (or they have too many possible meanings), and they have no obvious connexion with one another, or with what has gone before or what follows after. They come from a region of the mind where literal meaning does not matter and connexions may be still connexions even "without benefit of Reason". The old man is drawing upon memories of past experience and emotion, long ago put away and stored in the subconscious mind: and to draw them forth again he

[1] I use "stage-direction" loosely. Though no one really has the faintest idea what "Selah" means in the passages in the Psalms where it occurs, it seems most probable that it was a musical direction "To the Chief Musician". In that case it may have corresponded to our "tutti", or perhaps "ff": or it may have indicated (there are no limits to speculation) exactly the opposite, a General Pause: or . . . but this is not a treatise on Hebrew psalmody.

does not need to go to the trouble of making a strictly formal statement. He can do better. He needs only some powerful evocative word or phrase—which should be enough too for all but the most literal-minded reader, provided he will pause upon the phrase, and set his imagination free.

"Signs are taken for wonders." "We would see a sign!" Upon what memories is the old man drawing? That surely is not difficult. Upon his first religious experience: the beginning of it ("We would see a sign!" but God grants no special miracle even to the young and ardent): and the fruition. "The word within a word"—but there is neither need nor space to elaborate. So much is packed into each separate portmanteau. ("Word within a word," for instance. Amongst its innumerable other contents is the whole of the *Gospel of St. John*: "In the beginning was the word. . . . The word was made flesh.")

But, you may perhaps object, not without some show of reason—if one gives free play to the imagination and lets evocation work its will, can the result be anything but a hopeless muddle of unco-ordinated thought and image, a rabble without discipline or purpose? And how, you ask, remembering what you were taught at school, can a poem as a whole make sense without some sort of co-ordination amongst the parts?

This of course is perfectly true, as far as it goes. Free association, if you give it rein, both can and does produce a weird and wonderful assortment. Take, for example, one single line from the passage which we have just quoted above and unravel what is merely a fraction of the swarm of associations which it is intended to evoke.

The old man's thoughts, you realize, have gone back to his first religious experience, in his youth: which naturally suggests Springtime—" in the juvescence of the year". Like all religious experiences, which come when we are young and ardent, it was sweeping, over-mastering—like a tiger to its prey came Christ to the soul that was turning to Him.

> In depraved May, dogwood and chestnut, flowering
> judas. . . .

What comes out of this one line? This (and infinitely more)—The Christian ideal is ascetic, but the nature of youth is the opposite: it is full of passion and desire, like May, the spring-month of flowering: unrestrained luxuriant blossoming, sensuous and lovely, but depraved when contrasted with the restraint of passion which Christianity demands: in May flowers the wild-rose: and the chestnut: a flock of memories of such loveliness once seen and treasured comes nuzzling at the gates of the mind: in May too flowers the tree on which Judas is reputed to have hanged himself: Judas who betrayed his Master with a kiss: even so passion and desire betray me, make me traitor to Him. . . .

What connexion has this disconnexion?

If you mean connexion in the old sense of a direct coherent logical link between each of the several parts, there is none at all. This used to be regarded as one of the absolute essentials of all good writing—that any argument or story should proceed by logical steps to a logical conclusion. Incoherence (together with the obscurity which inevitably results from it) could only mean that something had gone wrong somewhere. That a writer should deliberately intend to be obscure was quite unthinkable! Either he must have failed to think out what he wanted to say, or he must have lacked sufficient skill to say it clearly. This of course is sound criticism and remains as true to-day as ever it was in the past—so long as one is dealing only with the conscious mind upon the surface; but what of the mind below? There, as we have seen in the last chapter, the writ of Reason does not run. Links need not be rational: opposite and incongruous thoughts lie down together, like the lion and the lamb. Any writer therefore, if and when he draws upon that reservoir, must say good-bye to logical connexion.

But connexion of some sort he must have. Otherwise what he writes will be no better than the ravings of a maniac. So in place of the logical he depends upon another kind of connexion altogether.

And of what kind is it? Mr. Day Lewis calls it "Emotional Sequence". "The reader," he goes on to explain,[1] "unaccustomed to the total absence of logical continuity is at first inclined to irritation. . . . Let him not overheat his intellectual bearings in an attempt to "think out" the connexions: the only entry into the position is an emotional one. If he will allow the images to cohabit in his mind for a little, he will find that a contact is made, a spark thrown off which illuminates the whole situation."

I do not altogether like the term "emotional sequence", though I admit that I cannot think of a better. It hits exactly the method of approach towards the understanding of this kind of poetry (Pause and

[1] *A Hope for Poetry*. Cecil Day Lewis. Pp. 20–1.

give Evocation time to do its work, " allow the images to cohabit in the mind "); but it implies that the conclusion, the " answer " to the addition sum, can be nothing more than a cloud of vague and indefinite feelings, which is all that can result from emotion alone. If that were all, you might reasonably wonder whether it would not be better to refuse to have anything to do with such poetry. Why wrestle with it, if you can expect nothing at the end but a confused and shifting chaos, like eddies of mist on a foggy morning? But you do expect and you do find a great deal more than that. The " meaning " of *Gerontion* is not so clear-cut and definite as the " meaning " of Browning's *Bishop*, but it is something much more definite than a cluster of indeterminate feelings. You " do " your sum without the help of logic: but to obtain the answer, some kind of thought, as well as emotion, is needed. You feel that you know the bishop, when you have done with him after reading the poem through. You feel also that you know Eliot's old man (perhaps not after reading the poem once or even twice), but it is with a different kind of knowledge: for you could not put the whole of what you know about him into words.

But—you may object again—how can anyone be said to know anything, if he is not able to say what it is that he knows?

This is a pertinent query, which in itself suggests a host of others. Does not knowledge depend on thought? And can one ever think without formulating in words the thought as it passes through the mind? Or do we " think in pictures ", as some of the psychologists assert? Or is all thought, as Plato insisted more than once,[1] a continuous monologue, exactly the same as speech except that it remains unspoken? And as for not being able to say what you know—can you even say that you have been thinking, if you find yourself unable to express the substance of your thought?—But this is philosophy's territory. We do not need to trespass on it or to involve ourselves in the mazes of the Theory of Knowledge. We can answer much more simply by considering the kind of knowledge which we have of our own friends.

Select any one from your circle of acquaintances, whom you believe yourself to know intimately. Take your pen in hand—or if you find it easier, speak into a dictaphone everything that you know about him (or it may be, her). In other words, compile a descriptive dossier as full and exhaustive as you please, even to the length of a five-volume novel—and what happens? However full you make it, however much detail of physical appearance or personal idiosyncrasy you can manage to put in, something at the end will still remain unsaid. I do not mean what always must escape you—that inner self which is every man's private possession and can never be wholly known to anyone except himself. I mean something which arises out of close familiarity and intimate acquaintance, which you feel you really know about your friend, although you may be quite unable to express it. I mean, in fact, in relation to a human being, what De La Mare says of the relation of all humanity to God in that very lovely little poem which

[1] Most explicitly, perhaps, in *The Sophist* (263 ad fin.) where the "Eleatic Stranger" makes Theaetetus agree that "thought is in no way different from speech, with this sole exception; thought is the unuttered conversation of the soul with herself".

is called *The Scribe.* I quote the latter part of it, not only because it is so apposite here, but for the pure pleasure of quoting:[1]

> Though I should sit
> By some tarn in thy hills,
> Using its ink
> As the spirit wills
> To write of Earth's wonders,
> Its live, willed things,
> Flit would the ages
> On soundless wings
> Ere unto Z
> My pen drew nigh;
> Leviathan told,
> And the honey-fly:
> And still would remain
> My wit to try—
> My worn reeds broken,
> The dark tarn dry,
> All words forgotten—
> Thou, Lord, and I.

What remains is definitely something, even though you might not be prepared to call it something definite: and it is something which you would claim to know.

So with the " meaning " of such poems as *Gerontion.* It is not a thing which can be caught and catalogued, pinned down and analysed to the last iota. On the other hand, once you have mastered the idiom and are content to let Evocation work its will upon you, you do not say at the end, " I have a kind of vague feeling. . . ." You say rather, " I can't put it all into words, but I do know what this poem means."

Take courage then. Accept Mr. Day Lewis's emi-

[1] The whole may be found in *Poems of To-day*, 2nd Series, No. 27; or of course in a volume of De la Mare.

nently practical advice and "do not overheat your intellectual bearings". Abandon logical connexion without a tear and cease to expect that two and two shall always equal four. In the world of mathematics this is fundamental: it embodies a principle upon which all calculation, and indeed all logical thought depends. But turn to the chemist in his laboratory and you enter a world where two and two quite possibly may equal five—or at any rate may result in the something which certainly is not four. Add hydrogen to oxygen, for instance, and you cannot work the answer out by mathematics. Yet it is a perfectly valid answer which we should all of us be prepared to accept. "Hydrogen plus Oxygen equals"—well, every schoolboy knows. . .

CHAPTER VIII

Note on Ezra Pound

ANYONE who reads *The Waste Land* will have noticed that it is dedicated to Ezra Pound, with the inscription

For Ezra Pound
il miglior fabbro.

Personally I think that Eliot is wrong—(he does not call him, you observe, " the greater poet ": only " the better craftsman ")—but that is a matter of opinion. Probably too most readers will be aware that neither Eliot nor Pound is English in origin: they are both American by birth. What then are they doing in our gallery of English poetry? Why should they figure in a book which does not profess even to touch upon the American poets of to-day and the interesting but quite different development of poetry in their hands?

It is a reasonable question; but there is a perfectly good answer. Both Eliot and Pound long ago shook the dust of their native country off their feet. The best part of their lives has been spent on this side the Atlantic, with the result that they have become if not cosmopolitanized, at any rate thoroughly and completely *déracinés*. Their " culture ", as Dr. Leavis would say, "is entirely European". Hence the frequent references to Continental literature in sundry different languages, which prove so disconcerting at times to readers without any Pentecostal gift. They have shed their American nationality altogether and their influence has been confined almost exclusively to our English poets; but upon them it has been very great indeed. We have already seen the extent and importance of the liaison between the French Symbolists and the New Movement in English poetry, when it was struggling to break away from conservative ideas and traditional methods. Pound and Eliot were the presiding geniuses at that rebirth. Their inclusion therefore in any account of modern developments in English poetry is not only justified: it is necessary and inevitable.

Pound is not negligible. Even if he wrote negligible poetry (which he certainly does not), it would be hard not to notice him. He takes good care of that. He can be on occasion strident and aggressive in his verse, though these moments of petulance are comparatively rare; but when he turns to prose (as he frequently does, to criticize, to exhort, and generally to fling his opinions in the face of the world), he makes himself as audible as an old-style sergeant-major. He writes, in fact, perpetually at the top of his voice, like the "barker" outside a circus-booth: or, to be more polite, his style has a kind of schoolboy exuberance, slangful and staccato, so that he always seems on the point of shouting "Yah!" and putting a derisive finger to his nose.

This method of argument attracts attention, if not respect. I should like to quote, if I had the space: for it would make extremely diverting reading. But we are concerned with Pound the poet: and here opinions differ very widely—all the way, indeed, from the laurel wreath to bell, book and candle.

Eliot prefixes to his volume of selections from

Pound [1] a long and discriminating critical introduction. It is the tribute of one poet of distinction to another, though by no means altogether laudatory throughout. " In some of the verse," he concludes, " I believe that the content is more important than the means of expression; in others the means of expression is the important thing; some combines both. . . . But," he continues, " concerning the contents of this book, I am quite certain of *Mauberley*,[2] whatever else I am certain of, this seems to me a great poem . . . it seems to me to be the verse of a man who knows his way about, to be a positive document of sensibility. It is compact of the experience of a certain man in a certain place at a certain time; and it is also a document of an epoch; it is genuine tragedy and comedy; and it is, in the best sense of Arnold's worn phrase, a criticism of life."

Contrast this with another estimate, no less incisive and no less definite. "Never has a man with less

[1] *Selected Poems*, Ezra Pound: with an introduction by T. S. Eliot.

[2] *Hugh Selwyn Mauberley*, to give it its full title. It is without question Pound's masterpiece—up to the point at which Eliot's volume of selections stops. (He includes nothing written since *Mauberley*, which was dated 1922.) It is a long poem made up of sections which are separate poems in themselves, yet each a contributory part of the whole. It might have been called " Ezra Pound revealed by Ezra Pound "; only it is more than that. It is at once a portrait by the author of himself and of the world in which he has lived (over a period ranging from the '90's to the closing stages of the War)—the whole being conveyed to you in the third person: the gradual disillusionment of one, Hugh Selwyn Mauberley, and his reactions to the obliquities of life as he finds it and sees it: and it is all done by oblique reference, never by direct statement—the " new technique ", in fact. In method it is the precursor of *The Waste Land*: and therefore as we have already discussed that poem very fully, I do not say anything further about *Mauberley* in this chapter—except that I think anyone who reads the poem carefully through (once and once again) and allows its sometimes not very obvious implications to grow upon him, will find himself at the end in agreement with Eliot's estimate.

talent and more charlatanry in his make-up succeeded in wielding so wide and pernicious an influence. Were it not that he is an American in London and so, though professing disgust with us as a nation of barbarians, an unsavoury example of what we as a nation produce, his doings would be of little moment. . . . He posed as a translator of the Chinese manuscripts of Fenellosa, was exposed as an ignorant fraud, and turned his hand to enlightening the Egoist followers upon the subject of Provençal literature. An authority on an old French and Provençal is compiling data from Pound's utterances which will expose Pound as utterly and incomprehensibly ignorant of the whole subject. One of Pound's recent preparations was a 'translation' of some poems by Propertius in *Poetry Magazine*. Dr. Hale of the University of Chicago in a letter reveals how little Pound knows of Latin. It is about time Ezra were put in the pound."

Obviously this is a blast of Transatlantic origin. (There is no love lost between the Simon Pure American on his native heath and his literary brother voluntarily expatriated in London or Paris.) It comes, as a matter of fact, from an "appreciation" of Pound which appeared in the *Chicago Tribune* in March, 1918, over the signature of a well-known and reputable critic.[1] Certainly 1918 is not exactly yesterday and certainly at that time *Mauberley* had not been completed in its present form; but you would have no difficulty to-day in finding quite a number of equally reputable persons to agree with every word. Indeed, Pound's latest

[1] Burton Rascoe by name. I take my information (and both quotations) from a most engaging and at the same time most instructive little book which has recently appeared: *Hold your tongue!* by Morris Ernst Alexander Lindey *Adventures* (as the sub-title explains) *in Libel and Slander*.

work (the *Draft of Cantos*, which is still in progress) has roused even greater controversy. Of these two voices, so flatly contradictory and yet each so positive, which is right? Or is it a case in which to take the middle way?

The American critic, when he wrote, knew nothing of the Cantos, just as he knew nothing of Mauberley; but it made no difference to him, when later he did. He remains implacably of the same opinion. As recently as 1932 he replied in public print to a particularly violent and provocative riposte of Pound's (also in public print) with the following amiable paragraph—" To be a clown is all right. To be a sophomore is all right. To be senile is all right. To be a senile sophomoric clown is obscene. Mr. Pound's case, however, is biologically interesting. Skipping the years of maturity, he passed imperceptibly from adolescence into second childhood. . . ." In other words, from the Pound of *Selected Poems* to the Pound of the Cantos.

Adolescence (which need not necessarily be a term of derogation) in the earlier poems we may admit. The titles alone of the various early volumes suggest a restless boy trying endless experiments: *Personæ of Ezra Pound*—*Ripostes*—*Lustra*—*Cathay*—you find them listed on the front page of *Selected Poems*. And indeed Pound has always been a kind of literary Proteus.[1]

[1] For the benefit of inexact scholars, the " Old Man of the Sea ": one of the few really reliable fortune-tellers in the ancient world, provided you could catch and hold him. He haunted certain definite localities in the Eastern Mediterranean and regularly came up about midday in one or other of them for a nap on the rocks. You stalked and caught him whilst asleep: he would then change in your arms into every form of animal known and unknown, returning at last, if you still retained your hold, to his original shape, which I imagine to have been something between a walrus and an Elder of the Tribe. After this final transformation he would reveal the shape of things to come.

Retrace the history of poetry since the '90's, the cliques, the coteries, the new movements that have started with a flourish and then died: you find that he has had a finger in them all. Evidence, you would say, of an original genius, an independent forward-looking and progressive mind? But read those earlier volumes through and you find also evidence (and plenty of it) of what is usually fatal to originality in a poet, except when he is young and in process of learning his trade. One expects "Juvenilia" to be reminiscent: even the great masters must write like someone else before they learn to write like themselves. But Pound's poetry, right up to *Hugh Selwyn Mauberley*, is reminiscent to a quite extraordinary degree. There is nothing faint or subtle about it, no dim distant echo: it is reminiscence as open and obvious as a full-blown rose. He is Whitman, he is Browning, he is Yeats—with a dash of Swinburne at times into the bargain.

These volumes are not Juvenilia: nor could they impress you, whatever your reaction to them otherwise may be, as the work of a mere imitator, or even a minor poet, fit only to hover on the edge of anthologies. Their author is so obviously a man who knows his own mind and has something definite to say. It is therefore very curious to find him so often writing with another's pen. But what is more curious still (and indeed contrary to all accepted rule), is this: blatantly reminiscent though he may be on occasion, it is rare to find a poem in which there is not something else—some other quality which one comes in time to recognize as peculiar to Pound.

Take for instance the little poem in *Lustra* called *Dance Figure for the Marriage in Cana of Galilee.* "In

Lustra," says Mr. Eliot in his introduction, "there are many voices"—but he will not allow that Whitman's is one of them. "It is indeed obvious that Pound owes nothing to Whitman. This is an elementary observation. . . ."

But consider the manner in which *Dance Figure* begins:

> Dark eyed,
> O woman of my dreams,
> Ivory sandalled. . . .

Is not this pure Whitman? But as it proceeds, gradually all trace of that rugged old sentimentalist disappears. A new and entirely different note begins to sound:

> Gilt turquoise and silver are in the place of thy rest.
> A brown robe, with threads of gold woven in
> patterns, hast thou gathered about thee,
> O Nathat-Ikanaie, "Tree-at-the-river".
>
> As a rillet among the sedge are thy hands upon me;
> Thy fingers a frosted stream. . . .

This is authentic Pound, and nobody else: an individual flavour—a kind of astringent honey.

But Browning Mr. Eliot will admit. "In the beautiful *Near Perigord* in *Lustra,*" he says, "there is the voice of Browning"—Indeed there is! *Near Perigord* is one of the fruits of Pound's researches into Provençal literature, about which Mr. Rascoe was so rude in the *Chicago Tribune.* It is a re-creation, a re-telling of a tale of Old Provence by a modern story-teller. It begins—can one mistake the manner? The bluffness, the heartiness, the familiar handling of mediæval names and personalities with which the ordinary reader is certain not to be familiar—

> You'd have men's hearts up from the dust
> And tell their secrets, Messire Cino,
> Right enough? Then read between the lines of
> Uc St. Circ,
> Solve me the riddle, for you know the tale.

You say to yourself, am I to be served with another Master Hugues, a Lippo Lippi, a second-hand draft from *Men and Women?* You are not: you may read on with confidence. The old story is brought to life in Pound's way, not in Browning's; and there is as much difference between them as between Scott's telling of Wandering Willie's Tale and a star reporter's version of it in a Sunday paper. You forget reminiscence in the rush and movement, the vividness and actuality of Pound's re-creation; and if as you read on, you stop to look for it, you find that it has disappeared. Eliot quotes the passage with which the poem closes: [1]

> There shut up in his castle, Tairiran's
> She who had nor ears nor tongue save in her hands,
> Gone—ah, gone—untouched, unreachable!
> She who could never live save through one person,
> She who could never speak save to one person,
> And all the rest of her a shifting change,
> A broken bundle of mirrors. . . .!

"These verses," he comments upon them, "are not Browning, or anybody else but Pound—but they are not the final Pound either. . . ."

And what is the final Pound, the last Protean transformation? Possibly *Mauberley* was the last but one,

[1] Poems from Lustra (1915), *Near Perigord*, III.

in which he turns suddenly and completely into a thorough-going Symbolist and all is inferential and oblique. And possibly the final stage (Proteus at last as himself) is to be found in the *Cantos*, that monumental Enigma which is still in process of construction.

It would be rash to prophesy. The *Cantos* are still appearing at irregular intervals, in irregular instalments. We are told that we are to have one hundred in all: and when they are complete, we are to be able to trace in the whole " a structure like that of a Bach fugue ".[1] We must wait in faith. At present they remain a gorgeous and exotic chaos, like a vigorous herbaceous border that has been allowed to run riot. Exactly what the final scheme will be, which is to co-ordinate all the parts and make the rough places plain, no one can possibly say—any more than given only one half of Joyce's *Ulysses*, anyone could confidently foretell the elaborate and detailed correspondence of the whole work with the structure of Homer's *Odyssey*.

The *Cantos* are obviously constructed upon a plan as elaborate as that of *Ulysses*: but speculation is idle until the fateful day on which the final instalment shall appear. Even Yeats, who has had the advantage of talking them over with the author, gives it up. " He is midway," he says in the introduction to *The Oxford Book of Modern Verse*, " in an immense poem in *vers libre* called for the moment *The Cantos*, where the metamorphosis of Dionysus, the descent of Odysseus into Hades, repeat themselves in various disguises, always in association with some third that is not repeated. . . . The relation of all the elements to one another, repeated or unrepeated, is to become

[1] *A Packet for Ezra Pound*, W. B. Yeats.

apparent when the whole is finished. There is no transmission through time, we pass without comment from Ancient Greece to modern England, from modern England to mediæval China; the symphony, the pattern, is timeless, flux eternal and therefore without movement. Like other readers I discover at present merely exquisite or grotesque fragments. . . ."

We may be content to find ourselves in such distinguished company.

This chapter is not intended as a critical essay, or any kind of comprehensive study. It is a Note rather (a Note of Interrogation perhaps) upon one of the most interesting, vivid and intriguing personalities in modern poetry. I shall therefore make only one further observation upon *The Cantos*.

They may or may not represent "the final Pound". Only time will show; but at any rate they include all the various Pounds that have appeared up to the present. They are not so much a new transformation as an assemblage of all previous transformations, welded together—one cannot say into one coherent whole, because no one yet knows exactly what that whole is intended to be; but one can say that they all contribute to the medley. And medley indeed it is! In *Mauberley* (as in *Gerontion* and *The Waste Land*) we abandon logical connexion. In *The Cantos* we let the time-sequence go as well. We rush up and down the centuries, with never a pointer, never even a wave of the hand to indicate "Change direction forward" or "Change direction back"; and continually, when our agility is being strained to the utmost, we have the added difficulty that the statement is not direct but evocative. Sometimes the clues to the evocation are simple or at any rate readily explicable by reference to dictionary or encyclopædia: as for instance, in the following passage from the beginning of Canto the Fourth:

> And by the curved, carved foot of the couch, claw-foot and
> lion head, an old man seated
> Speaking in a low drone. . . .
> Ityn!
> Et ter flebiliter, Ityn, Ityn!
> And she went toward the window and cast her down,
> " All the while, the while, the swallows crying: Ityn!
> It is Cabestan's heart in the dish."
> " It is Cabestan's heart in the dish?
> No other taste shall change this."
> And she went towards the window. . . .

This is comparatively straightforward though there is a jump without warning from ancient Greece to old Provence. The old Greek legend of the boy Itys served up as a dish for dinner to his father drifts almost imperceptibly into the equally grim and equally cannibalistic Provençal tale. If you are not familiar with them already, you have only to look up [1] the two stories in a work of reference and the whole becomes clear.

But the clues to evocation (and likewise the transitions in time) are by no means always so simple. Often —indeed, almost as often as not—the reference is a fragment from some little-known writer of no particular distinction, whom few would go to the trouble of read-

[1] And further to realize that Pound is taking the Greek story from Ovid's version of it in the sixth book of his *Metamorphoses*. Hence " et ter flebiliter Ityn "—the swallow (or rather Itys' mother, later changed into a swallow)

> crying thrice with tearful voice
> Itys, Itys. . ..

ing, and fewer of remembering: or it may be a piece of slang, a colloquial tag in some foreign tongue (he has a repertoire of eight languages, ancient, mediæval and modern, with some of which, one suspects, he is more familiar than others): or maybe it is a phrase, a saying, a quotation, of which the application presumably is crystal-clear to Pound himself but at first sight very much the reverse to anyone else. Indeed it often seems that if any outsider should succeed in battling through to comprehension, it must be rather by divine dispensation than human ingenuity.

Take, for example, Canto the Twenty-sixth (we must summarize, since it is too long to quote in full). It begins with a reminiscence of modern Venice: passes without warning into mid-fifteenth century and a minor incident in Venetian history—(a flashlight picture of mediæval manners, brief as the burning of a magnesium powder: you must be quick to catch what you can of it while the light lasts): glances at the murder of Lorenzo dei Medici a hundred years or so later: touches on the troubles of a hard-working artist (not so much difference between Venice then and St. John's Wood to-day): and closes with an echo of Mozart's famous row with the Archbishop of Salzburg. The actual conclusion is one single line, between inverted commas, standing in isolation. It runs thus:

> As is the sonata, so is little Miss Cannabich.

What relevance can the ordinary plain reader hope to find in this, even if he is familiar enough with the detail of Mozart's life to be able to " place " the lady?

One must admit that such " private " or semi-private references, occurring so constantly, are, to say the least, somewhat discouraging; and when you add to these the numerous obscure and recondite allusions (which look at times suspiciously like deliberate displays of out-of-the-way unusual learning [1]) you might well be tempted to give up in despair. On the other hand, one must admit also that it is not all complication,

> dark involution and sense of veil'd import.

More often than you might suspect, you come upon stretches of indubitable poetry, as simple and straightforward as anyone could wish: immediately recognizable as such, without need of any unusual knowledge or special ingenuity in interpretation.

We may close our "Note on Pound" with one example:

> Within her cave, Nerea,
> she like a great shell curved
> In the suavity of the rock,
> cliff green-gray in the far,
> In the near, the gate-cliffs of amber,
> And the wave
> green clear, and blue clear,

[1] I think it is fair to remark that Pound's learning is most in evidence in fields in which recognized scholars have been least active and least interested. Some would say that this is only natural, since originality never follows the beaten track: others would give a different explanation. We may content ourselves with an example. The first *Canto* is a rescript, a re-creation of the beginning of the eleventh book of Homer's *Odyssey* (ll. 1–153). It announces one of the recurrent themes which are to make up the "pattern of the fugue": what is commonly referred to as the "Descent of Odysseus in Hades" (though as a matter of fact, he went no further than the edge of the Underworld and employed the ancient method of materialization by the shedding of fresh blood). But is it upon the celebrated and immortal original that Pound bases his reconstruction? It is not—as we are told at the end of the *Canto*. He is paraphrasing a paraphrase made by one, Andreas Divus in the sixteenth century; and if you find (as I think you do find) that he has missed some of the best things in Homer's version, he can always reply, "Ah, but that's Divus! I don't expect you have ever heard of him. . . ."

And the cave salt-white, and glare-purple,
    cool, porphyry smooth,
    the rock sea-worn,
No gull-cry no sound of porpoise,
Sand as of malachite, and no cold there,
    the light not of sun. . . .[1]

No learning is needed here: only to read and let the gracious rhythm take you, and enjoy.

[1] Canto, XVII, *ad init.*

CHAPTER IX

The Sitwells

MENTION modern poetry in general company—at a dinner-party, say, if the atmosphere seems not too unfavourable—and nine times out of ten the response, if there is any at all, will be a somewhat tentative, " Oh—ah—yes. The Sitwells I suppose you mean? . . ." (unless of course someone particularly up-to-date gets in first with " Auden—Spender—Lewis "). Press further and you may elicit a still more tentative, " Difficult stuff! And isn't it recited? To a flute and a drum: or something of the sort? And that extraordinary new music!"

And if the papers, as is their habit at regular intervals, decide to revive that evergreen controversy, the Old versus the New (" Poetry is poetry no more ")—how long is it before the name of Sitwell inevitably crops up in the argument?

In fact, I imagine, if one could take a general census, our best-known modern poet is—" The Sitwells ".

Miss Edith Sitwell in the introductory essay to her brother Sacheverell's *Collected Poems* claims him outright as " the poet who is, to my mind, one of the greatest that our race has produced in the last hundred and fifty years." This is a high claim. The " last hundred and fifty years " would take us back to Burns and Blake; and after them the whole Romantic Epoch follows, a period as crowded with great names as any in the history of our literature. Even if, following the present fashion, you eliminate the Victorians in a body, there are still left Coleridge and Wordsworth, Byron and Shelley and Keats.

It is a high claim indeed; but Miss Sitwell is herself a poet of considerable distinction. She is also a critic whose tongue is possibly the most flaming and scarifying in our generation. It would be neither possible nor politic to set aside what she so emphatically asserts, without most careful examination.

And Yeats too in his Introduction to *The Oxford Book of Modern Verse* (that curious parti-coloured hybrid, "out of Prejudice by Critical Acumen") is very definite in his appreciation, though he displays more caution and pitches his praise on a note less high. He is speaking of Binyon and Sturge Moore (both of them, we may notice, poets who belong wholly to the Georgian tradition). "Their fame," he says, "will increase with time. They have been joined of late years by Sacheverell Sitwell. . . ."

Such tribute is impressive. Let us then split the Trinity, the composite poet of general renown: and put, as does Miss Sitwell, her brother Sacheverell first. "This great poetry," she says of his work, "whose rhythms are those of growth, of the birth and death of the seasons . . . the extraordinary variation of these rhythms, the equally amazing sensuous beauty of these poems. . . ."

It is, I think, beyond question true that if you were compiling an anthology of lovely lines and passages from English poetry (the kind of book that used to be so popular for keeping by the bedside, entitled *A Garland*, or its modern counterpart, *A Week-end Book*), you could fill quite a large section with excerpts from

Sacheverell Sitwell; and what is more, that section would rank amongst the best and loveliest in the whole collection. Take, for example, this from *Variations on a Theme by Marlowe* (which Miss Sitwell herself selects for quotation in her introductory essay):

Come now, my halcyon, I call you back,
Come from the bough, there, that your weight sags down,
And float to my feet so that I smooth your plumes!
Tell me, where does air lie softest,
In the West round the sun, or do the stars ride calm,
Their lamps burning level, never shaken in the tide?
He peered in every corner and he chose the West,
And running to my feet he shook his wings and glittered. . . .

Or this, from *Agamemnon's Tomb*: storm over the Peloponnese: you are looking down from the hill-fortress of the ancient Achæan kings eastward over the plain of Argos:

The climb to Mycenæ, when the wind and rain
Stormed at the tombs, when the rocks were as clouds
Struck still in the hurricane, driven to the hillside,
And rain poured in torrents, all the air was water.
The wet grey Argolide wept below,
The winds wailed and tore their hair,
The plain of Argos mourned and was in mist,
In mist tossed and shaken, in a sea of wrack.[1]

Or this, of music after the feast in the great hall of the Abbey of Thelema:

Music opened its winged moods for them,
Floating, half in heaven, half on earth, as did that swing
Which dropped a golden nymph, and drew her back again
Until that thing of melody, that lovely body,
Fell like a fruit into the lap of grass.[2]

[1] *Canons of Giant Art. Agamemnon's Tomb.*
[2] *Dr. Donne and Gargantua,* Canto the Fourth, *in med.*

Or a single line:

> These madrigals of water and the leaves' bright lutes. . . .[1]

One could go on diamond-digging indefinitely, but a string of excerpts, however charming and felicitous, does not of itself make a major poet. To be convinced, one must take the poems as a whole—or rather certain poems whole: selecting of course the best, the richest cream from the top of the bowl. For it is upon this, the best of which a poet is capable, that his real quality must be assessed. The remainder, wherever he falls short of his own highest standard, does not matter to this kind of judgment at all, since it is only the essentially mediocre who succeed in maintaining one consistent level throughout.

Let us then take Mr. Sitwell at his best. We have already quoted a fragment from *Agamemnon's Tomb*: but now consider the poem as a whole. It is well worth consideration. Miss Sitwell herself expressly refers to it in her Introduction as "to my mind, one of the greatest poems in the English language for over a century:" the same bold claim which she makes for her brother as a poet earlier at the beginning of her essay.

And how, on examination, does the poem stand up to it? Let us see.

Agamemnon's Tomb is the fifth of a series of entirely separate poems grouped together under the title *Canons of Giant Art*.[2] It is written, as they all are, in that "Sprung Rhythm", which we have already noticed

[1] *Dr. Donne and Gargantua*, Canto the Fifth, *ad fin.*

[2] Not a conspicuously illuminating title: (did he choose it for its unusualness, to arrest attention, or simply out of "cussedness"? The sub-title, however, *Twenty Torsos in Heroic Landscapes*, explains (if you give yourself time to think it out) a little more clearly the scope and intention of the work.

in our second chapter as dis-interred and re-introduced into English poetry by Gerard Hopkins. (Each line, you remember, is made up of a fixed number of stresses, themselves of indeterminate length.) It is a meditation upon the age-old theme of Mortality and Death: the occasion being a visit to the burial-place of the great king who once led all Greece crusading into Asia.

> Tomb

it begins (a full echoing line, one single word long):

> A hollow hateful word
> A bell, a leaden bell the dry lips mock
> . . . a sink of damp and mould, that's all,
> Whose bones make dust and move not otherwise;
> Who loves the spider or the worm, for this,
> That they starve in there, but are its liveliness?

This is the theme upon which the poet lets loose his ingenious and macabre imagination. The detail of Death obsesses him—what comes before

> the miser hand
> That clutches at an edge of wood, a chair, a table,
> Must have its fingers broken, have its bones cracked back,
> It's the rigor mortis, death struggle out of life. . . .

and what follows after

> What dreams must they have who die so quiet in sleep,
> What dread pursuings into arms of terror,
> Feared all through life, gigantic in dark corridors. . . .

And so he proceeds, pursuing the implications of his theme through all the convolutions that a most unusual intellect and an equally unusual imagination can suggest.

It is like Donne: only it has a smoothness which Donne never managed to achieve. It is like Poe: only it never takes you to the edge of that nightmare world where sanity and reason fail and you can hear the monkey-chatter of what is not human.

We come at last to Mycenæ and the tomb:

> The wind shrieked, the rain poured, the steep wet stones
> Were a cliff in a whirlwind, by a raging sea,
> Hidden by the rainstorm pelting down from heaven
> To that hollow valley loud with melancholy;
> But the dark hill opened. And it was the tomb.

The tone of the meditation changes. It becomes less macabre: ingenuity is less at strain.

And so to the solemn and sombre close—

> Listen, listen, listen to the voice of the water
> Alive and living, more than Agamemnon,
> Whose name is sound of footsteps on the shaking boards,
> A tragedian's ghost, a shadow on the rocks.
> You are dead, you are dead, and all the dead are nothing
> to it,
> There's nothing, nothing, nothing, not a breath beyond:
> O give up every hope of it, we'll wake no more,
> We are the world and it will end with us:
> The heart is not a clock, it will not wind again,
> The dead are but dead, there is no use for them,
> They neither care, nor care not, they are only dead.

This is poetry: and fine poetry—but is it major poetry? For that and no less is what Miss Sitwell claims.

" Great is the confusion," she says at the beginning of her introductory essay, " as to the needs of poetry in this age, and this confusion arises from a muddle-headed conception, on the part of certain critics, that a poem is of no importance unless it voices some purely contemporary feeling or problem, or produces a photographic representation of some contemporary theme." It is not difficult to guess to whom Miss Sitwell is referring; but she has named no names and neither need we. Of course it is a stupidity to suppose that poetry, in order to have significance, must concern itself exclusively with contemporary problems or contemporary ideas; and it is more than a stupidity to imagine that a photographic reproduction of anything can be poetry at all. Art, whatever view you take of it, must depend to some extent upon the individual outlook and imaginative insight of the artist.

But to say this is not to say that poetry need have no connexion at all with contemporary life. Connexion of some sort there must be. The poet is of his age. He lives in it, whether he likes it or not: and when he writes, he writes primarily for his own age and not for some distant and more sympathetic future. (Even the most superior and self-sufficient of our Intelligentsia are not entirely above caring whether anyone reads them or no.) Actually it is upon this connexion that the distinction between merely good and really great poetry in the last resort depends. What makes the difference is not choice of subject or felicity of language or anything of that kind (in all these the lesser man may equal the master): but it is the breadth and the depth of the poet's understanding of human nature—which he can only get from observation and experience of the world in which he lives.

Supposing a poet turns from to-day and tries to live wholly in yesterday—supposing even he only shuts himself off from certain parts of life as it presents itself to him, his poetry is bound to lose in significance. Either it must be minor poetry, with nothing in it (to use a horrid phrase beloved of certain modern critics), "to impinge upon the consciousness of the present generation"; which being interpreted means that it will lack reality and substance, like Mr. Wells's Pycraft who for all his outward bulk could not prevent himself from floating to the ceiling. Or—it may not be minor poetry, but something very much better. It may attract enormously at first reading and almost it may convince, so that you are prepared to exclaim with enthusiasm, "this is the real thing!" But on reflection you find yourself left with an uneasy suspicion of something wanting—"so near and yet so far". The reason is, of course, that the poet is not speaking out of a broad and general experience, which is yours and mine and every man's as well as his own, but out of a private world, largely peculiar to himself in which the reader cannot fully share. It may be a world of great beauty, of infinite subtlety and almost irresistible charm. Nevertheless it has no real spaciousness: it is as much a *hortus inclusus* as the little world inside a monastery wall, which is by no means co-incident with the larger world outside.

Apply this now to the case of Mr. Sitwell. No one would suggest that *Agamemnon's Tomb* is minor poetry —but poetry from a private world is a different matter. Take up the poem again and read it through: up to the point at which the meditation ends and the description of Mycenæ begins. At first you are perhaps too captivated by the endless flow of the melodious brook to take account of what it has been saying to you; but forget the music for the moment. Stop your ears against the siren song, and dispassionately reflect. Actually how much has been said? In one sense, a great deal: one hundred and sixty-nine lines of it, in fact. (I have been to the trouble of counting them, since there is no numbering in the text.) But how vital is it all? How nearly does it touch your own experience?

There is more in poetry than sound alone. There is meaning: and the meaning of great poetry grows upon you, like a rocket expanding in the darkness. It discovers affinities in the reader's mind, it awakens echoes so that one says, "he is speaking to me and in a sense he is speaking for me". . . . But is this the impression which *Agamemnon's Tomb* leaves upon you? Do you, after it is all over, feel that intimacy of connexion? I think not. I think rather that you feel you have been privileged to look over the wall and watch one of the most supple and graceful of acrobats performing marvels of ingenuity in his own private garden.

Miss Sitwell herself gives the case away. She quotes [1] *in extenso* an early poem—but we need only the first eight lines:

> The gold voice of the sunset was most clearly in the air
> As I wandered through the outskirts of the town.
>
> And here dispersed upon the grass, I see
> Confetti-thick the amorous couples—
> What thoughts, what scenes, evoke, evaporate
> in leaden minds like theirs?
> Can I create them? These things
> which mean the happiness of multitudes. . . .

"He is accused," she says, "by the Bungalow

[1] *Collected Poems*, Sacheverell Sitwell, Introductory Essay, p. 32.

School[1] of inhumanity. . . . But can it really be claimed that this poem, written by a twenty-year old poet of genius, is inhuman?"

I think no one would go so far as that: certainly not after reading the whole poem. On the other hand, there are very definite limits to its humanity. How superior is the reference to "the amorous couples, confetti-thick"! And how "precious" is the latter epithet! How aloof, how external is the poet as he observes! How carefully, like the Levite, he passes by on the other side! Is it not clear that even thus early the young man is preparing his private world? Deliberately rejecting, in fact, a large portion of human experience. . . . One cannot avoid thinking of the social snob who deliberately limits the circle of her acquaintance—"Oh, that Miss Jones! My dear, I simply couldn't know her!"

Miss Sitwell's own poetry is harder and crisper, less garrulous and less grandiose than her brother's. It may not reach his standard at his best; but it is certainly more widely read and more generally known.

It is of two kinds: recognizably related but very different. The more usual (which for most people represents the typical "Sitwell") is bright and brittle. It leaves you with the impression of an elaborate Crystal Palace, innumerable surfaces of glass reflecting

[1] In the ranks of "The Bungalow School" Miss Sitwell includes in one comprehensive damnation all those who hold that poetry's proper place is in the market-place and not Pegasus-riding after Beauty in the clouds.

She would remind them that there are parts of the market-place which are drab and dreary, and parts which are sordid and malodorous.

They would remind her of a famous line in one of Terence's plays (with which she is not likely to be unfamiliar)

> Homo sum: et nihil humani alienum a me puto.
> I am a man: and all humanity is my proper province.

at innumerable angles—or perhaps you are reminded of nothing so objective. One should say rather that it resembles Sacheverell's halcyon:

> And running to my feet he shook his wings and glittered.

He flashes, he fascinates, he dazzles—but could anyone mistake him for a real and genuine bird? One accepts him for what he is: a creature of the world inhabited by the gryphon and the wyvern and the strange fowl that stands upon the pinnacle of the Liver Building.

Miss Sitwell writes as deliberately from a private world as does her brother; and it is a world even more private, more separated from the ordinary world of men and women than his. *Colonel Fantock* is perhaps a fantasy; but there is autobiography in it too, if you do not press for facts too hard.

> Thus spoke the lady underneath the trees
> I was a member of a family. . . .

So it begins. And the family consisted of two brothers and a sister:

> Dagobert and Peregrine and I
> Were children then. . . .
> And life still held some promise—never ask
> Of what—but life seemed less a stranger, then,
> Than ever after in this cold existence.
> I always was a little outside life. . . .

And so she writes—as if she were "always a little outside life". The effect is of extreme brilliance and at the same time of extreme artificiality.

"A modern writer," says Yeats in his Introduction to *The Oxford Book of Modern Verse*,[1] "may escape

[1] Introduction, p. XIX.

into the classics . . . or with much loss of self-control and coherence may force language against its will into a powerful, artificial vividness. Edith Sitwell has a temperament of a strangeness so high-pitched that only through this artifice could it find expression. . . ." "Nature," he says later (still speaking of Miss Sitwell and her poetry: I think, with invincible justice), "appears before us in a hashish-eater's dream. This dream is double; in its first half, through separated metaphor . . . she creates, amid crowds and scenery that suggest the Russian ballet and Aubrey Beardsley's final phase, a perpetual metamorphosis that seems an elegant, artificial childhood; but," he continues, "in the other half, driven by a necessity of contrast, a nightmare vision like that of Webster, of the emblems of mortality. . . ."

This is Miss Sitwell's other side. Possibly it is the better and will prove more lasting. Certainly it is the more understandable and puts fewer difficulties (of forced language, strained and distorted metaphor, fantasy stretched to its most fantastical) in the way of the reader. Indeed at her best in this vein, she is almost simple: and consequently there is none of that "loss of self-control and coherence" which Yeats justly condemns in the other.

That remarkable study in Grand-Guignol, *The Hambone and the Heart*, combines both Miss Sitwell's manners—most conveniently for our observation, since they are not mixed but separate, like the strata of a Neapolitan ice. It is a gargoyle of a poem, powerful, macabre, curiously wrought almost to the point of a grotesque. It opens to a theme similar to that of *Agamemnon's Tomb*, but treated with a terseness and a bareness very different from Sacheverell's ample flowing opulence:

> That terrible Gehenna of the bone
> Deserted by the flesh—with Death alone!

Death and Mortality are symbolized under the figure of a Hambone, rotten with corruption, held in the hand of a clown. All this first part, together with the epilogue at the end, is in Miss Sitwell's most " Sitwellian " manner: highly fantastical, speaking through symbols that stand at several removes from reality, " language forced against its will. . . ."

> Like little pigeons small dove-breasted flowers
> Were cooing of far-off bird-footed showers,
>
> Beneath the twisted rose-boughs of the heat
> Our shadows walked like little foreigners,
> Like small unhappy children dressed in mourning,
> They listened by the serres-chaudes waterfalls
>
> There by the waterfalls we saw the Clown,
> As tall as Heaven's golden town,
> And in his hands, a Heart, and a Hambone. . . .

But the middle section is a short story: complete in itself and capable of standing by itself, a little masterpiece of story-telling. For myself, I could wish that it did stand alone; but Miss Sitwell has given it a connexion both with prologue and epilogue. The " Heart " is symbol for all that is opposite to the Hambone: it stands for human love and human aspiration and human hopes; and it is the Heart that now speaks. What befalls love and aspiration and hope in the world of men? You are to see in the story which follows.

Actually the Heart speaks through the mouth of a mother, resting without rest in her grave:

> For they lie
> Who say the Dead can ever die.

She had an only son and had given him her all: starved herself, even, at times for him. He grows up and turns to another—and younger woman. He must have money to meet her demands: and there is only his mother's tiny store of savings which she keeps under her bed. Finally he kills his mother for that money. She hears his step by the bed, wakes and meets his eye, just as the knife falls. The conclusion is masterly—what the mother thinks, as she lies, resting without rest:

> The life-blood that my son's hand shed—
> That from my broken heart outburst,
> I'd give again to quench his thirst.
>
> He did no sin. But cold blind earth
> The body was that gave him birth.
> All mine, all mine the sin. The love
> I bore him was not deep enough.

This has the swift direct simplicity of the best of the old ballads. It is strong, because it is bare. Miss Sitwell has altered her manner to suit her subject. She has forgotten to be fantastical: there are no "dove-breasted flowers" and no "bird-footed showers". She is concerned only with telling her story, without adornments and without complications. In consequence, the effect is immediate—and tremendous, since there is no eccentricity of thought or language to stand between the reader and the writer's intention. When

Miss Sitwell writes like this, the question of artificiality does not even arise. Simplicity need not always be naïve: it may be, as in *The Heart and the Hambone*, highly sophisticated; but it still remains simplicity.

There remains the third member of the trinity, Mr. Osbert Sitwell. He too is a poet of no negligible quality (you find him scattered up and down the anthologies); but he writes better a charming, sensitive and delicate prose.

CHAPTER X

William Butler Yeats

THERE still remains one imposing and arresting figure.

Mr. Yeats's position in the world of poetry to-day is both outstanding and unique. His eminence is undisputed. Actually all the warring sects regard him with respect, from the reactionary to the progressive (even to the last word in modernity). "New Verse," which is normally as little respectful as a lower schoolboy to anything outside its own pet prejudices, speaks of him as "an accepted poet, though belittled and misunderstood". And at the other end of the scale, the B.B.C. announces a talk by him as from "our leading authority upon Poetry". Indeed, if you were to name him anywhere as our greatest living poet, I doubt whether you would find one voice raised in opposition.

But, for all this general acceptance, he stands in a curious isolation. He has no definite following, no body of disciples to call him "Father", like the group which surrounded Ben Jonson: he has not even a swarm of imitators trailing after him. He has not introduced into English poetry any startling new methods: and he has not "invented" any special technique which can be recognized as peculiar to himself. You need no lexicon or commentary to help you to understand him. Yet his influence upon the poets of the New Movement, from the time of its inception down to the present day, has been nearly as great as that of Eliot and Hopkins: not so direct, or so immediately obvious; but if you look for it, it is there—even in the most unsuspected places.

He is, moreover, a veteran—born, to be precise, in '65, the year in which appeared Matthew Arnold's first series of *Essays in Criticism*: which makes it all the more remarkable that he should be held in such esteem by the younger generation, who are less inclined now than perhaps at any time to regard the Elders of the Tribe with any sort of veneration. Long before the New Movement was ever dreamed of, and before the Indian summer of the Georgians, he was a figure in the world of letters—writing in the '90's the kind of poetry which the '90's expected. Without clairvoyance you could no more foretell his present stature than you could divine the later Tennyson in the gushful inepti-tudes of *Where Claribel low lieth.*

George Moore in the first volume of *Hail and Farewell*[1] has a portrait of the Yeats of the early days (drawn with that accurate malice of which Moore was a master). " It is true that when I saw him he was on exhibition " —the occasion was the first performance of Yeats's *Land of Heart's Desire*—" striding to and forth at the back of the dress circle, a long black cloak drooping from his shoulders, a soft black sombrero on his head, a voluminous black silk tie flowing from his collar, loose black trousers dragging untidily over his long, heavy feet—a man of such excessive appearance that I could not do otherwise—could I?—than to mistake him for an Irish parody of the poetry that I had seen

[1] *Ave*, p. 45.

all my life strutting its rhythmic way in the alleys of the Luxembourg gardens . . ."

Reading his early poetry, we might almost make the same mistake. It belongs to its period: and furthermore, in contrast to the poetry of his maturity, it belongs to a definite school. " I was in all things Pre-Raphaelite," he says of himself in the *Auto-biographies*. And so he was—in intention; but when it came to expressing himself, the voice is just a little different from the typical voice of the '90's:

> Had I the heavens' embroidered cloths,
> Enwrought with golden and silver light,
> The blue and the dim and the dark cloths
> Of night and light and the half light . . .

Yeats of course is Irish, born and bred, and soaked in Irish tradition (which accounts for much subsequently in his life and his opinions). Consequently in the '90's, though he speaks good late-Victorianese, he speaks it with an Irish accent. Not that he lapses into brogue or employs a synthetic dialect, as did J. M. Synge. It is his rhythms that are different. They are not the stereotyped conventional rhythms of the poetry of that day, but the free natural cadences of his native folk-song which he brought with him from the west of Ireland.

It was Arthur Symons who first made known in this country the work and gospel of the Symbolists in France—doing for them on a lesser scale what William Archer about the same time was doing for Ibsen. Through Symons, Yeats made acquaintance with the Movement thus early in its history: and later (at some time early in the '90's) in Paris met Mallarmé, arch-priest of the cult. That meeting, one cannot help reflecting, was itself symbolical in the true "Symbolist" sense: a fit subject for Max Beerbohm's inimitable pencil. It is not difficult to imagine what he would have made of it—and underneath, the caption "Dream meeting Dream" . . .

Yeats already had much in common with the Symbolists. Both aimed at something elusive and intangible: both were subjective, alike in method and natural mode of thought: both were essentially fantasist. But you do not find (as you might perhaps expect) that acquaintance with them made any radical difference to his poetry. Symbolist ideas profoundly affected and attracted him, as may be gathered from the *Auto-biographies* and his other very candid accounts of his own mind and its development. "It seemed to me at the time," he says, "the only movement which was saying new things." Yet no one ever thinks of Yeats as primarily a "Symbolist" poet, and he certainly did not inspire any new movement in the '90's along Symbolist lines. As to his own poetry of that period—there is no essential difference in form or method between *The Wanderings of Oisin* of 1889 and *The Wind among the Reeds* of 1899.

He had no need to copy the poets across the Channel.

Their aim, as we have already seen in a previous chapter, was indirection. There are so many things even in our ordinary experience either too complex or too fragile to be properly expressed by plain direct statement. ("How shall the thick finger not bruise the miracle of the butterfly's wing?") Mallarmé even, according to Valéry who succeeded him in the priesthood, "never discussed his ideas except figuratively he had a curious repugnance to explaining anything in direct words." That may have been a peculiarity of Mallarmé's peculiar temperament; but it was also the logical outcome of Symbolist theory. And of course to a certain extent everyone would agree. When Blake wrote:

> Tyger, Tyger, burning bright
> In the forests of the night . . .

in those two lines he said more of the vastness and grandeur of God's creation, man's insignificance, and Nature's terrifying magnificence than he ever could in a hundred pages of explanatory prose. The symbol, instantly apprehended by every reader, is an amplifier of infinite range. But the difficulty with the Symbolists was that they saw no need to make their symbol either simple or universal. A poet was at liberty to choose arbitrarily at his own discretion whatever he liked. Thus anything might stand for anything: a boot for a broken heart, Circe's hair for artistic perfection, sundial inscriptions for the business of practical life.[1]

But Yeats, long before he became acquainted with the Symbolists, had brought with him when he left his native Ireland a whole bagful of symbols of his own. The Irish mythology is as rich in great stories and great figures as the Icelandic and, almost, as the Greek: and equally rich is the borderland where myth and history meet. It was upon this inexhaustible store that he drew for symbol—to make up " that phantas-

[1] *Hugh Selwyn Mauberley*. Ezra Pound. *Ode pour l'élection de son sépulcre*—

> He
> observed the elegance of Circe's hair,
> Rather than the mottoes on sundials.

magoria ", as he says in the Preface to *The Wild Swans at Coole*, " through which I can alone express my convictions about the world ". The figures in the phantasmagoria may be little more real than the symbols of the French poets; but at least they are not figments of one man's imagination or individual caprices of one man's invention. Generations have gone to their making, and they enter Yeats's text, like Wordsworth's infant, trailing clouds . . .

At times we may be in danger of losing ourselves among the clouds. For the difficulty with this kind of symbol is that few of us have Yeats's familiarity with Celtic lore. It is not always easy to find one's way through the Ferguses and Ænguses, the Danaan children, white deer without horns, boars without bristles, and all the rest; and further, he has a most aggravating habit of mixing without warning characters of his own invention with this legendary and heroic company.

The only excuse for symbol is that something vital about human life can be better or more fully said in that way than in any other. The danger of it is that it affords one of the easiest means of escape into the lotus-land of unreality. And all Yeats's poetry, until the moment when he sets foot on the road to Damascus, is a Poetry of Escape. It is poignant: much of it is as haunting as a lovely tune. At the same time it is curiously indefinite and unsubstantial, like a mirage in the clouds—and sometimes one wonders if he has not mistaken the symbol for the reality for which it stands.

He describes himself at this period with great candour and insight at the beginning of *The Trembling of the Veil*. " I was," he says, " unlike others of my generation in one thing only. I had made a new religion, almost an infallible church, of poetic tradition, of a fardel of stories, and of personages, and of emotions, inseparable from their first expression, passed on from generation to generation . . . I wished for a world, where I could discover this tradition perpetually, and not in pictures and in poems only . . . I had even created a dogma: 'Because those imaginary people are created out of the deepest instinct of man, to be his measure and his norm, whatever I can imagine those mouths speaking may be the nearest I can go to truth.'"

Is not this the perfect portrait of an inveterate Escapist? Is he, you must wonder, any more—certainly he is not less—than the Dreamer of his own very lovely and defeatist little poem, *The Man who dreamed of Faeryland*?:

> He stood among a crowd at Drumahair;
> His heart hung all upon a silken dress,
> And he had known at last some tenderness,
> Before earth made of him her sleepy care;
> But when a man poured fish into a pile,
> It seemed they raised their little silver heads,
> And sang how day a Druid twilight sheds
> Upon a dim, green, well-beloved isle,
> Where people love beside star-laden seas;
> How Time may never mar their faery vows
> Under the woven roofs of quicken boughs:
> The singing shook him out of his new ease . . .

He was, of course, more—even at the time at which this was written. "There has always been," Mr. Edmund Wilson justly remarks in his chapter on Yeats in *Axel's Castle*, "more of the public figure and more of the pugnacious Irishman about him than his philosophy invites us to believe."

Remembering Moore's picture of him at the first night of *Land of Heart's Desire*, one might easily forget that his connexion with the theatre was by no means confined to the writing of verse-plays for it. He was more than the figurehead: he was the leading figure throughout in the long campaign for the establishment of a National Theatre in Dublin; and it was due to him, at least as much as to Lady Gregory, that in the end it was established. "I have spent much of my time," he says in his account of it in the volume of collected papers called *Plays & Controversies*,[1] "and more of my thought these last ten years on Irish organization, and now that the Irish Literary Theatre has completed the plan I had in my head ten years ago, I want to go down again to primary ideas . . ." In other words, the poet prepares to go back to his proper job: "I hope to get our heroic age into verse, and to solve some problems of the speaking of verse to musical notes . . ." But such was not to be. The infant, once born, needed constant care and attention from its parents. He nursed it and he fought for it: he wrote for it and he spoke for it (as of course did Lady Gregory too); but again it was due to him, at least as much as to her or to Miss Horniman, that the National Theatre survived the storms and troubles of its early years . . .

The story of the Abbey Theatre is a little epic of courage and vision, triumphant over every kind of prejudice and obstruction. It has been told by many, from various angles. Yeats has told it at first hand from his: and Moore, who left the ship almost before she had started on her voyage, has mocked at it from

[1] *Plays and Controversies.* W. B. Yeats. "The Irish Dramatic Movement", p. 9.

his. But all that is outside the scope and purpose of this chapter. It concerns us here only as evidence that the "Man who dreamed of Faeryland" had another and quite unexpected side. Vision you would grant, but courage you would hardly gather from that early poetry. Escape is a form of evasion: a man looks up to avoid looking down at the unpleasant things that lie before his feet. That needs no courage.

But when you turn to the mature and later Yeats, you find both these qualities in combination. No longer are they kept, so to speak, in separate compartments—the vision for the making of poetry: the courage for the business of living. They are fused, they work in partnership together; and it is this combination of the two that transforms him from the dream-singer of the '90's into the major poet that he is to-day.

The change came somewhere in the early years of the century. We might attempt to date it—but what are dates? A man does not change his whole outlook in a day. It was a gradual conversion. Take *The Wind among the Reeds* of 1899, or *Cathleen ni Hoolihan* of 1902, and contrast them with *The Green Helmet* which appeared in 1910. The difference is radical.

The earlier Yeats, the Yeats of *Aedh wishes for the Cloths of Heaven,* had been a spinner of words: the master of a style as mannered and as ornate in its own way as Swinburne's or Rossetti's: not so rich and not so heavy-loaded: simpler, but so carefully worked over that every simplicity seems calculated (as indeed it was). But now all that disappeared. "I found that without knowing it," he said in *Discoveries* (midway through the period of the change), "I had come to care for nothing but impersonal beauty.

I had set out on life with the thought of putting my very self into poetry and had understood this as a representation of my own visions and an attempt to cut away the non-essential, but as I imagined the visions outside myself my imagination became full of decorative landscape and of still life. The more I tried to make my art deliberately beautiful the more did I follow the opposite of myself."

One of the objections to modern poetry most commonly heard is that the poets will not take the trouble "deliberately to make their art beautiful". "It may be clever," say the lovers of poetry (when it is poetry), "and it may be as progressive as you like—but there's no beauty in it. That's a thing nobody seems to care about any more!" But the poets do care; only they think of it in a different way. The fact is, Beauty (with a capital B) by the end of the nineteenth century had become a fetish: "a principle", according to the second meaning given in the Oxford Dictionary, "irrationally reverenced"—and "excessively" reverenced, we might add. It gave the Escapists such a magnificent excuse for mounting their horses and riding off into the clouds: for there, and only there, so they alleged in their own defence, away from the ugliness and imperfections of ordinary and common contemporary life was the object of their quest to be found. They had forgotten that Keats once wrote:

Beauty is Truth . . .

or rather they had never understood what he meant: that the whole truth about life is beautiful, provided it is the truth, and a man if he has vision discovers it, so to speak, on his own doorstep, not in the clouds.

You may look up to heaven in your search for it; but if you refuse to look down again at the human muddle at your feet, it will be nothing but an "impersonal beauty" that you will achieve. And that, for a poet, means exactly that loss of touch, that atmosphere of unreality, which drove Modern Poetry into revolt.

Yeats himself is an object lesson. There is his earlier poetry: so haunting and so lovely, but at the same time so self-conscious and so artificial. None of it, even the best, entirely convinces you. Take that speech of Oona's with which *The Countess Kathleen* ends:

> Tell them who walk upon the floor of peace
> That I would die and go to her I love;
> The years like great black oxen tread the world,
> And God the herdsman goads them on behind
> And I am broken by their passing feet.

When I was sixteen, I thought that great poetry. I had not the penetration to see how consciously elaborated it is, and how much of the beauty which it undoubtedly has depends upon the care with which it has been beautified.

But turn from this to his later manner. Turn, for example, to the sheer naked simplicity of the opening of *The Tower*. There is no conscious beautification: its beauty lies in its truth and sincerity:

> What shall I do with this absurdity—
> O heart, O troubled heart—this caricature,
> Decrepit age that has been tied to me
> As to a dog's tail?
>   Never had I more
> Excited, passionate, fantastical
> Imagination, nor an ear and eye
> That more expected the impossible—
> No, not in boyhood when with rod and fly,

> Or the humbler worm, I climbed Ben Bulben's back
> And had the livelong summer day to spend.
> It seems that I must bid the Muse go pack,
> Choose Plato and Plotinus for a friend
> Until imagination, ear and eye,
> Can be content with argument and deal
> In abstract things; or be derided by
> A sort of battered kettle at the heel.[1]

The power of this poetry lies in its bare austerity. In it, Vision to see beyond appearances and courage to see without evasion are met together. It has no tricks. It belongs to no school. He has freed himself from *Innisfree*: and refused to run his head into the mazes of Canto-land. All his early work aimed at reaching reality through dream. That failed, because he found himself losing touch with life: "I had come to care for nothing but impersonal beauty . . . Decorative landscape and still life." Now in his maturity he has discarded all that heroic dream-world of legend and faery: and seeks for reality, where it really is, in the contemporary world of men. In consequence it is poetry of profound disillusion:

> The Holy Centaurs of the hill are vanished;
> I have nothing but the embittered sun;
> Banished heroic moon and vanished,
> And now that I have come to fifty years,
> I must endure the timid sun . . .

There is no bird, as D. H. Lawrence said in a different connexion, to put a song into the throat of morning.

But all the first-class poetry of this present age is poetry of disillusion, and we have already seen the

[1] *The Tower*, title-poem of the present volume of that name, which, together with *The Wild Swans at Coole*, contains, I think, Yeats's supreme achievement as a poet.

reason why. In a time of flux and change and constant movement, when Certainty has been destroyed and the old standards shaken and the new not yet proved and tested, the poet has no choice. He must voyage over the moving waters, like the dove out of the Ark: and report, if he is honest—" not yet any place to settle, nor yet any dry land on which to rest ".

Nevertheless there may be Vision even without certainty.

EPILOGUE

OUR Key has, I hope, now served its purpose. It was not meant to do more than unlock the door of the " Room of Modern Poetry ", and at the same time provide a kind of bird's eye view of the exhibits inside. You will now know something of their history and their background: at least I hope so. You will know something about their divisions and connexions, the different groups into which they are split up: and (what is most important for proper understanding) something about the reasons why they are what they are—or in less polite language, " how they have got themselves into such a state ".

You may perhaps wonder at certain omissions. What of so-and-so? you say, picking on a poet whom you are willing to recognize as a poet: is he not an outstanding figure? And so-and-so, is he not worthy even of a mention? But, let me remind you again, this book was not intended as a textbook or a history. There are of course several poets of real importance and distinction whom we have not noticed; but their omission was deliberate. They do not come within the general scheme.

There is De La Mare, for instance. In any detailed account of English poetry to-day he would have high place. He is the singer of the world behind the world, and the realities of Childhood, shorn of adult sentiment and the falsities of wish-fulfilment glamour. The result is that he is curiously remote and yet curiously real. His magic can be white, as we have seen in *The Scribe* (quoted at the end of Chapter VII); but it can be dark and sinister too. *The Mocking Fairy*, for example, is a study in the uncanny only sixteen lines long, but as powerful and disturbing as any of his ghost stories at greater length in prose. It begins, as perhaps you remember, in seeming childlike innocence:

> "Won't you look out of your window, Mrs. Gill?"
> Quoth the Fairy, nidding, nodding in the garden,
> "Can't you look out of your window, Mrs. Gill?"
> Quoth the Fairy, laughing softly in the garden . . ."

and mounts through every degree of apprehension and unease to the sheer horror of its conclusion.

> And out of her cold cottage never answered Mrs. Gill
> The Fairy mimbling mambling in the garden.

And there is W. H. Davies. His concern is with the ordinary world around us. "A plain man," he calls himself:

> This Davies has no depth,
> He writes of birds, of staring cows and sheep,
> And throws no light on deep, eternal things . . ."

but he makes of every common experience he touches something deep and rich and rare. He too has two manners:

> While joy gave clouds the light of stars,
> That beamed where'er they looked:
> And calves and lambs had tottering knees,
> Excited, while they sucked;
>
> . . . .

I turned my head and saw the wind,
Not far from where I stood,
Dragging the corn by her golden hair,
Into a dark and lonely wood.[1]

That is one: the other you will find in sardonic little poems like *The Inquest*. An unmarried mother's child has died and the Coroner sits with a jury. What verdict shall they find? Finally, to "Death by Misadventure".

"Aye, aye," said we. The mother smiled . . .

And the little story ends (all its sting in its tail):

And I could see that child's one eye
Which seemed to laugh, and say with glee:
"What caused my death you'll never know—
Perhaps my mother murdered me."

These are two poets whom it is impossible to overlook. They both belong essentially to To-day: there is no suspicion of Yesterday about them. They speak the crisp and terse language of the twentieth century: they reject no part of contemporary experience, but at the same time they are both essentially individual and self-contained. In consequence neither has any specific place in the story of the development of poetry in this modern age: both are outside the purpose of this book. Like A. E. Housman (who in every word he wrote was never anything but completely *sui generis*), each inhabits his own world in undisturbed and undisturbing isolation, islanded, you might say, amidst the eddies of the twentieth-century stream.

And should you feel disposed to count Housman as one of our omissions, since he died only recently and

[1] *The Villain*, W. H. Davies.

his last volume[1] was published as late as 1922, the sufficient answer is that he excluded himself. "I can no longer," he wrote in the Preface to *Last Poems*, "expect to be revisited by the continuous excitement under which in the early months of 1895 I wrote the greater part of my other book, nor indeed could I well sustain it if it came . . ." He could not. Whatever other qualities he had—and they were many—he had no forward look. *Last Poems* covers the same ground as *A Shropshire Lad*: and covers it less well. That earlier volume of the middle '90's remains his masterpiece—and his monument.

And there are the younger poets, the true "children of the twentieth century", born to the unrest to which the pioneers, their elders, have had perforce to adjust themselves. When you leave the vantage-post at the door and step inside the "Room", you will find them all there waiting for you: and that is the proper place for detailed discussion of them. This book has only been intended to enable you to meet them on something like equal terms.

But perhaps before we finally part company and say good-bye, there is one little group of three whom we ought just to notice. They will certainly be amongst the first with whom you will make acquaintance, when you step inside the "Room". Probably you know something of them already, beyond the glimpses we have had of them from the doorway standing—outstanding, rather one ought to say—with faces gallantly, if a little theatrically, turned to face the future. Their names are Auden, Spender and Day Lewis.

I do not propose to discuss them in any detail. You

[1] *More Poems*, the last volume of all, was a posthumous collection.

will find plenty of critics doing that inside the Room (including themselves: for they are always ready to talk about themselves). I mention them now only, as it were, to effect an introduction.

Since Eliot after *Ash-Wednesday* withdrew into *The Rock* and similar austerities, they are the leading members of that modern group which (as we have seen [1]) Miss Sitwell calls the *Bungalow School*. They are anathema to her—and worse: for their view of poetry and its function is almost completely the opposite of hers. "The difference," she says in speaking of her brother,[2] "between his poetry and the verse produced by the Bungalow School is this: his poetry is formed of beauty: beauty is the air in which it moves—and their verse . . . !" But for them beauty is not the poet's only, or even his supreme aim. They believe that the poet's business is primarily with his contemporary world, not to isolate what beauty there may be in it, but to report the whole truth about it as he sees it. Art for them is Communication of Truth: not only factual truth, but that further truth which only vision can discern. "Behaviour," says Spender,[3] "lags behind the immediate processes of life, which are concerned with what people really believe, and which are the subject of poetry. Poetry is sensitive to new forms of life, long before they have influenced behaviour."

This is their Creed (or one of the fundamentals of it). In this belief they are one, though it is a triumvirate rather than a trinity. They may be generally thought

[1] Vide note to p. 147.
[2] Introductory Essay to *Collected Poems of Sacheverell Sitwell*, p. 34.
[3] *The Destructive Element*, Stephen Spender, p. 203.

and spoken of together as a group; but each is entirely distinct and individual, with a style and method and manner peculiarly his own, as you will find when you make closer acquaintance with them at first hand.

Auden, for instance, you could not mistake for Spender, still less for Day Lewis. Turn to his poetry and you find a curious creature. Take his early volume and gather from it himself as he was up to 1930.[1] Unmistakably there is in it a genuine poet of sensitiveness and considerable imaginative power: with a crisp, concentrated, at times almost tabloid, style of his own. Consider, for example, this:

> Time passes in Hessen, in Gutensberg,
> With hill-top and evening holds me up,
> Tiny observer of enormous world.
> Smoke rises from factory in field,
> Memory of fire: On all sides heard
> Vanishing music of isolated larks:
> From village square voices in hymn,
> Men's voices, an old use.
> And I above, standing . . .[2]

But there is also in the book (and equally unmistakably) a clever young man who, one suspects, rejoices in his frequent obscurities and is prepared at any moment to fob the reader off with empty conceits and scarcely worth-while clevernesses, which are sometimes not clevernesses at all:

> The silly fool, the silly fool
> Was sillier in school
> But beat the bully as a rule.

[1] *Poems*, W. H. Auden. " I have omitted," he says in a Note to the second edition, " certain poems which were printed in the first edition. The poems substituted for them were all written before 1931."

[2] *Poems*, No. XVI.

The youngest son, the youngest son
Was certainly no wise one
Yet could surprise one.

Or rather, or rather
To be posh, we gather,
One should have no father . . .[1]

The proper comment upon this is best out of print.

But six years later a second volume appeared, which contains the deliberately selected best of his work in the interval (since the *Poems* of 1930). In it the clever young man who was often so astonishingly crude has almost disappeared. (Actually, I think, he migrated to the theatre, succumbing to the poet's standing temptation to become a "writer of plays". In my opinion he is much in evidence both in *The Dance of Death* and *The Dog beneath the Skin*: but that of course is only an opinion.) This later volume is a great advance upon the first. It is stronger, deeper, warmer. The style, which you will have come to recognize as his from the earlier poems, still remains the same, crisp and concentrated and bare; but it has to a large extent lost that extreme and exaggerated staccato which was at times so irritating and could be so befogging. Compare, for instance, the title-poem, *Look, Stranger!* No. V, of the second volume with *It was Easter when I walked in the public garden*, No. XVI of the first, from which we took our first extract above. You see the same individual manner, but smoothed and mastered. There is no word too much, but now there is no word too little:

[1] *Poems*, No. XIX. There are six more lines of it.

Look, stranger, at this island now
The leaping light for your delight discovers,
Stand stable here
And silent be,
That through the channels of the ear
May wander like a river
The swaying sound of the sea.
. . . .
Far off like floating seeds the ships
Diverge on urgent voluntary errands;
And the full view
Indeed may enter
And move in memory as now these clouds do,
That pass the harbour mirror
And all the summer through the water saunter.

This is indisputable poetry, as genuine as Stephen Spender's *Express*, but quite distinct and different.

We have already quoted from *The Express* (at the end of Chapter VII), as illustrating the modern poet's familiarity with the awkward new modern things: how naturally and without effort he takes them and makes poetry out of them. " Mr. Auden's poems and Mr. Day Lewis's *From Feathers to Iron*," Michael Roberts rightly observes in the Preface to *New Signatures* (though curiously he omits Spender), " were, I think, the first books in which imagery taken from contemporary life consistently appeared as the natural and spontaneous expression of the poet's thought and feeling . . ."

Feathers to Iron is a long poem (twenty-nine separate poems long, in fact), celebrating the emotional experience of the young husband—any young husband, though the poem in form is autobiography—from marriage to the birth of his first child. It proceeds in sequence from the " Feathers " of the first cloudy ecstasy through the deep waters of the woman's labour to the "Iron" of a true and tested spiritual understanding, when the child is safely born. It is a record of emotions, which can only express themselves through imagery. We have seen how the old poetic tradition practically obliged the poet in his search for metaphor and image to confine himself to "Nature", or at any rate to things "hallowed by custom and venerable from much use". We have seen also how the New Movement in poetry broke away from that tradition. The modern poet, glancing "from heaven to earth, from earth to heaven", has immeasurably increased his range. He has added to the store from which he draws his metaphor and his images the whole civilized and sophisticated life of modern man.

We might answer the strictures of Miss Sitwell and other critics upon the Bungalow School with a question. Need "beauty" vanish, provided the poet is completely at his ease and takes, so to speak, the modern material in his stride? If anyone thinks so, let him then consider the following two stanzas from the song of victory with which *From Feathers to Iron* ends:

> Now shall the airman vertically banking
> Out of the blue write a new sky-sign;
> The nine tramp steamers rusting in the estuary
> Get up full pressure for a trade revival;
> The crusty landlord renew the lease, and everyone
> Take a whole holiday in honour of this.
>
> . . . .
>
> Wherever radiance from ashes arises—
> Willow herb glowing on abandoned slagheaps,
> Dawn budding scarlet in a bed of darkness,
> Life from exhausted womb outstriving—
> There shall the spirit be lightened and gratefully
> Take a whole holiday in honour of this.

Or let him consider . . .

But we started out to say a brief good-bye: and like two ladies parting on a doorstep, we have taken far too long over saying it.

Let us say so now, before we are tempted to speak beyond our brief.

INDEX

CHELTENHAM PUBLIC LIBRARY